# FAIL-SAFE INVESTING

How You Can Profit from the Coming Devaluation (1970)

How I Found Freedom in an Unfree World (1973, 1998)

You Can Profit from a Monetary Crisis (1974)

New Profits from the Monetary Crisis (1975)

The Complete Guide to Swiss Banks (1976)

Inflation-Proofing Your Investments (1981, with Terry Coxon)

Investment Rule #1 (1985)

Why the Best-Laid Investment Plans Usually Go Wrong (1986)

The Economic Time Bomb (1989)

Why Government Doesn't Work (1995)

# FAIL-SAFE INVESTING

### Lifelong Financial Security in 30 Minutes

## Harry Browne

ST. MARTIN'S GRIFFIN ⚞ NEW YORK

www.stmartins.com

Book design by Richard Oriolo

Library of Congress Cataloging-in-Publication Data

Browne, Harry.
    Fail-safe investing : lifelong financial security in 30 minutes / Harry Browne.
        p.  cm.
    Includes index.
    ISBN 0-312-24703-6 (hc)
    ISBN 0-312-26321-X (pbk)
    1. Finance, Personal.  2. Investments.
I. Title.
HG179.B7478  1999
332.024—dc21                                    99-15902
                                                 CIP

First published in the United States under the title *Fail-Safe Investing: Lifelong Financial Safety in 30 Minutes*

D 10 9 8

To Pamela, Sable, and Candy

# Contents

## Part II: **More about the Rules**

## Appendices

# Prologue:

# Keep It Safe
# and Simple

The investment world can seem to be a mysterious place—filled with moving averages, IPOs, reverse spreads, stochastics, a "Footsie" index, the Fed "injecting" and "draining" liquidity, and more ratios than you might care to hear about.

I entered that world in the 1960s and set out to understand it all. But the more I learned about sophisticated techniques, supposedly savvy strategies, and the secrets of the very rich, the more I came to understand that the real secret of investing is just this:

*Keep it safe and simple.*

This book will show you how to do so—how to handle your investments with minimum effort and no worry, and yet make sure your wealth (however large or small) is safe and growing.

## Two Worlds?

You earned the money you've accumulated by using common sense to provide a service others were willing to pay for.

Most likely, that same resource of common sense has led you as well to friendships, romance, and the emotional maturity that allows you to enjoy life. Wherever you go, whatever new challenge or problem you face, you fall back on your common-sense understanding of how the world works. You should be able to use that understanding in investing just as well.

But many—if not most—financial experts and advisors talk as though the investment world were somehow different from the rest of life. They divine the future from lines and squiggles on charts, as though they were witch doctors examining entrails. Or they base their strategy on mob psychology, as though human beings were all dunderheads who can't think for themselves.

This is where the trouble begins. You might think you've entered a parallel universe controlled by prophecy, mysterious symbols, obscure cycles, and strange ideas about how human beings behave—everything you'd shun if the topic weren't investing, and if the hope of big gains didn't cloud your common sense.

Such strange ideas about how the investment world works can divert you from the simple, straightforward principles that have led to your success in everything else you've done.

In truth, the investment world is a part of the same world you already know and deal with successfully. And your common sense is far more valuable to you than all the jargon, analyses, and trading systems you hear about.

## The 17 Simple Rules

Unlike most investment books, this one won't teach you a secret theory of investing. Instead, it presents 17 simple rules that will remind you of what you already know and give you the confidence to act on that knowledge.

These rules will protect you against the unreality prevalent in so much writing and conversation about investing. The rules will ensure that your investments will enhance your life and will grow into a safe and comfortable retirement. And they will make certain you don't lose your hard-earned money.

The rules won't make you privy to the secrets of the world's greatest speculators—but nothing else you read will do that, either.

Your reaction to some of the rules may be "Of course, that's obvious." But the obvious is precisely what you must cling to—and it's what too many financial writers will try to separate you from. Danger lurks wherever you reach for exotic and complicated concepts—disregarding the plain truths that have brought you this far in life.

In Part I, we will look at the 17 rules. Since most of them are largely self-evident, they require very few words to explain. You can read through all the rules in 30 minutes or less.

Part II provides background information and some not-so-obvious examples of heeding or ignoring each rule. Refer to Part II for more explanation or if you're not sure how to apply a rule.

While the rules are largely warnings to exercise prudence, they won't stop you from making profits. They even leave room for trying to strike it rich with part of your money, if that's what you want to do. But their first job is to keep you from making any mistake that could be financially fatal.

Investing doesn't have to be difficult, dangerous, complicated, or mysterious. It demands only that you relax and keep your head, that you approach the investment world in the same way you've handled the rest of your life—even if everyone you know chooses not to.

These rules are by far the most important truths I've learned in my 30 years in the investment world. They have made money for me, they have kept my investments safe, and they have made my investment life simple.

In the next 30 minutes you'll have the benefit of my 30 years' experience, so that the rules can do the same for you.

Part I

# The
# 17 Simple Rules
# of Financial
# Safety

# Build Your Wealth
# upon Your Career

Working together, your career and your investments can build a prosperous, secure future. But never forget that your wealth begins with your career—the way you make your day-to-day living.

If you save enough from your business, profession, or job, you eventually may earn more from investing than from working. But unless you first pay attention to working and saving, you'll never share in the wealth that investing can bring.

You might see advertisements claiming that investing just a few thousand dollars will put you on the road to riches. But investing is the second part of the road. The first part is the money you earn and save from your job. Rarely does someone make a large fortune from investments alone.

And common sense tells you it has to be this way.

Think about your own occupation, for example. Could someone without your training, your skills, your experience, and your talent outperform you at your job?

Of course not.

And yet too-good-to-be-true advertisements invite you—an amateur with no particular education, training, or experience in speculation—to compete, in your spare time, with professionals who have devoted their entire careers to investing, and who continue to eat, breathe, and sleep investing every day.

The sad fact is that most part-time investors who try to beat the markets lose part or all of the savings they've worked so hard to accumulate. Some of them wind up using their working income to cover investment losses—and maybe even working overtime to do so.

When the quick-money approach does produce gains, the profits usually are smaller than if you had simply made a few conservative investments and left them alone.

*Could you beat the pros by reading a book or a newsletter?*

You tell me. Did Luciano Pavarotti become the world's leading tenor by studying a book? Did Babe Ruth learn to hit home runs by subscribing to a newsletter?

*Can you make big profits by relying on an expert who does have the proper qualifications?*

How do you identify a true expert? That task is no easier than picking the right investments. If you don't understand investing as well as the pros, you won't know how to evaluate those who seek to advise you. And you can't rely on an advisor's track record, even when it's presented honestly. Track records tell you only how advisors did in the past—not how they will do next year.

## Violating the Rule

You're violating Rule #1 if you think your investments can be the sole source of your retirement wealth—or if you steal time from your work to manage your investments—or if you think about abandoning your job to become a full-time investor.

## Why You Must Invest

Does this mean you can't achieve anything by investing?

No, quite the contrary: Investing can do so much for your future that it would be a terrible shame to squander its true opportunities by chasing after rainbows.

Investing wisely can amplify and enhance what you earn by your labor. And it is the only thing you really can count on for your senior years. You can't depend on Social Security to take care of you.

Social Security operates on a simple principle:

*You give your retirement money to politicians and they squander it on something else.*

They may spend it on someone else's retirement—or on building monuments to themselves—or on programs to curry re-election support from special-interest groups. But the one thing they will never do is put your money in a trust fund earmarked for your retirement.

Social Security operates on a basis that would send the owners of any private insurance company to prison: It expects to repay your "contribution" with money it will take from someone else later. As the years pass, it becomes harder and harder to keep this pyramid scheme going.

The system will be reformed someday—and perhaps even completely taken away from the politicians. But the sad and silly history of politics warns us that real reform won't happen until the system is close to collapse. In the meantime, the only changes will be to reduce benefits, delay the retirement age, or increase taxes.

The closer you are to retirement now, the bigger chance

you have to get something back from Social Security. But, in general, the safest way to consider the matter is to assume you won't get anything—and then treat anything you receive as found money.

You can count on for your retirement only what you put away yourself. And you must make sure that what you put away is safe and growing at a healthy rate.

Fortunately, if you handle your investments properly, you *can* count on them to finance your retirement—and more. And the younger you are, the easier it is to provide a good retirement—and the less reason you have to worry about Social Security.

## Benefits of Investing

If you apply common sense, your investments can:

1.  Assure you of a secure and comfortable retirement.
2.  Enhance your life before then—perhaps by providing a better home, a better education for your children, or whatever may be important to you.
3.  Allow you to leave something substantial for your heirs.

Investing won't promote you from the middle class to the very rich. Most people who hoped it would do so have wound up worse off. So don't take risks with complicated investment schemes in the hope of multiplying your capital quickly.

Instead, set up an investment plan:

- That protects and enhances what you've earned at your job, and

- That isn't so complicated you'll be tempted to abandon it.

In other words, keep it safe and simple.

If you do that, you'll be free to concentrate on what you do best—free to make a great deal of money in your career.

# Don't Assume You
# Can Replace Your Wealth

If risky investments turn out badly and you lose everything you have, you might be able to earn it all back again. But don't count on it.

Yes, you know far more now than when you started your career, but success always depends on conditions you don't control. And those conditions are constantly changing. Markets change, technology changes, the competition changes, consumer tastes change, and laws and regulations change.

You earned your wealth because your talent and effort harmonized with the circumstances in which you found yourself. But the world won't stand still for you or repeat itself when you need it to.

As time passes, government finds new ways to interfere with your business, your profession, and your life. Expanding regulations and the litigation explosion combine to make businesses much more vulnerable today to surprises and sudden disasters. And advances in technology change the demand for your products or service.

So assume that what you have now is irreplaceable, that you could never earn it again—even if you suspect you could.

Recognize, too, that without prudence whatever wealth you've accumulated is vulnerable to the same kinds of surprises—litigation, regulation, investigation, market setbacks, changing tastes, or just plain misjudgment. So you need to find a way to protect your savings from every eventuality—a task that, fortunately, isn't as daunting as it might seem.

You're violating Rule #2 any time you think it's okay to go for broke with the savings you're counting on for the future—or when you treat your wealth with anything other than the utmost respect.

Protecting what you have requires setting up an investment program whose first priority is to preserve what you've worked for—making sure you don't take chances with the part of your wealth that's precious to you.

No matter how much or little you have now, it's possible to assure that you'll never lose it—as we'll see in Rule #11.

But the first step is to recognize how precious your wealth is, and resolve to say "No!" to any proposition that asks you to risk losing it.

**RULE #3**

# Recognize the Difference between Investing and Speculating

Investors often get into trouble by speculating when they think they're investing. If you don't understand the difference between the two, you can put yourself in a dangerous situation.

When you invest, you accept whatever return the markets are paying investors in general.

When you speculate, you attempt to beat that return—to do better than other investors are doing—through clever timing, forecasting, or selection. The implicit assumption is that you have knowledge or talents other investors lack.

You're investing when:

- You hold a long-term position in the stock market with no attempt to time your investments or to determine which sectors of the market will perform best.

- You keep your savings in a money market fund or a bank account.

- You hold a balanced portfolio, with a variety of investments, so that at least one will do well—and keep your portfolio afloat—in any economic climate.

You're speculating when:

- You select individual stocks, mutual funds, or stock market sectors you believe will do better than the market as a whole.

- You move your capital in and out of markets according to how well you think they'll perform in the near future.

- You base your investments on current prospects for the nation's economy.

- You use fundamental analysis, technical analysis, cyclical analysis, or any other form of analysis or system to tell you when to buy and sell.

Investment advisors and writers often refer to "safe investments" when they're really talking about speculations. And no matter how they assure you that a given speculation involves little risk, it is still a speculation.

The distinction between investing and speculating is important. Any attempt to beat the return available to others must, by definition, also involve the risk that your return will be smaller than what the market is offering effortlessly—or even that there will be no return at all.

As we proceed, I hope you'll see why I want you to understand the difference between investing and speculating. Both are honorable endeavors, but only one of them is suitable for the funds you're basing your future on.

There's nothing wrong with speculating—*provided you do it only with money you can afford to lose*. But the wealth that's precious to you—the money you're counting on for retirement—should never be risked on a bet that you can outperform other investors.

# Beware of Fortune-Tellers

We live in an uncertain world.

Whenever you make a decision—whether in your business or personal life—you're always dealing with incomplete knowledge. You may make the best choice you can, but you know you can't control the actions of other people. Nor can you know for sure how other people will react to future events.

That doesn't mean you can't make sensible decisions, can't succeed, or can't live a happy and prosperous life. Even though you can't *eliminate* uncertainty, you know there are ways to deal with it. In fact, you have dealt successfully with uncertainty in amassing the money you now have to invest.

Because no psychic or seer can tell you what the future holds, you make decisions in your business and personal life using whatever knowledge is available. Respecting uncertainty, you make choices that let you capitalize on opportunities, but with safeguards that protect you from being hurt too badly if things don't turn out as expected.

You take a job knowing that tomorrow's economic conditions may eliminate the company's need for what you do. Or you start a business with no guarantee that the marketplace will be kind to you. You marry, acquire friends, pick a place to live—all without any certain knowledge of how your choices will turn out.

Most of us live that way—and live well. You would never rely on someone who claimed to predict the outcome of these activities. It wouldn't make sense.

You know that if someone *could* predict the future, he'd be off somewhere making billions of dollars betting on sporting events or advising corporate giants—not offering his predictions to you for $100 or so.

Most people understand that true seers don't exist in the real world.

## Forsaking What We Know

And yet, when contemplating your investments, it's easy to think you must find a fortune-teller with an outstanding "track record"—one who can predict future stock prices, next year's inflation rate, or the direction of gold prices.

You won't have to look very far to find someone who claims to have a foolproof way to know which way the markets are moving. The investment world is overpopulated with seers who claim to have amazing forecasting records.

But you'll find that the advisor with a perfect forecasting record up to now will lose his touch the moment you start acting on his advice.

Investing is no different from the rest of life. Investment prices flow from the decisions of millions of different people. Investors and advisors have no more ability to foresee those decisions than psychics or fortune-tellers do.

As with the rest of your life, safety doesn't come from trying to peer into the future to eliminate uncertainty. Safety comes from devising realistic ways to deal with uncertainty.

You're violating Rule #4 if you believe a certain event *has* to come about—or that a given investment can't fail—or that you have good reason to know that some apparent risk simply won't materialize—or that someone out there knows which way the market will move next year.

The truth is simply that:

*Anything* can happen.

*Nothing* **has** to happen.

The beginning of investment wisdom is the realization that we live in an uncertain world—and that *no one* can eliminate the uncertainty for you.

Once you recognize that simple truth, you will look for ways to assure that the uncertain future won't hurt you—no matter *what* it turns out to be.

Then you'll be able to relax, free from worry that future surprises could destroy your savings—no longer afraid that you may act on the wrong prediction.

In Rule #11, we'll see how you can handle uncertainty.

# Don't Expect
# Anyone to Make
# You Rich

Perhaps it *is* unrealistic for you, investing part-time, to expect to outdo the professionals. But couldn't you beat the game by using a professional's advice?

If you read many investment publications, you could easily conclude that this is what you should do. There are plenty of stories about Wall Street wizards who can get you into and out of investments with skillful timing. And so many of them seem to have outstanding track records.

But I hope you'll heed what others have learned the hard way:

> *The investment expert with the perfect record up to now will lose his touch as soon as you start acting on his advice.*

Investment advisors come in many garbs—such as stock and commodity brokers, newsletter writers, financial journalists, money managers, and financial planners.

No matter what their occupational titles, they fit into two groups:

- *Helpers:* People who use their knowledge and experience to help you set up an investment portfolio that suits your needs, and to show you how to carry out your plans.

- *Market-Beaters:* People who recommend speculations to help you obtain a greater return than the markets are offering to others.

Of course, some advisors do both.

## Helpers

The Helper is worth listening to. He or she can acquaint you with investment alternatives you weren't aware of, and that might be a good fit for you. He can teach you the mechanics and procedures for getting things done in the investment world. He can raise the questions you need to answer in order to devise a portfolio that suits your needs. He can help you reduce the tax bill on your investment profits.

## Market-Beaters

A Market-Beater does something else. He points to speculative opportunities you might not otherwise see, identifies the risks involved in a speculation, and even keeps you humble by pointing to possible future events you haven't allowed for.

But, no matter how smart or experienced he is, the Market-Beater can't predict the future. Nor can you expect him to spot the right times to buy and sell reliably. No one can, because no one can know the motivations and intentions of hundreds of millions of different people—each of whom will have an effect on next month's prices, and each of whom can change his mind in unpredictable ways.

Not surprisingly, most Market-Beaters claim to have made lots of money for their customers. And each generally provides a sterling track record—whether precise or informal.

But the future is a different story. Somehow the record isn't as good once you're acting on the advice.

That doesn't mean no Market-Beater is going to do well next year. Some of them may have spectacular years. But, obviously, not all of them will—no matter what their records—and there's no way you can know in advance which one is going to have a good year.

## Coincidence and Luck

It's easy to assume that an advisor with a good recent record is the best choice. After all, he's the one with the "hot hand" right now. But his recent record may reflect nothing more than a brief lucky streak—one that's about to end.

When you hear of someone who has just made several "uncanny" recommendations in a row, think how you'd respond to news elsewhere in your life that someone has performed miracles. You'd know that coincidence, luck, or some other overlooked possibility probably explains what people are calling miraculous. You should apply that same skepticism to similar tales in the investment world.

The common rebuttal is that there have been too many successes to be mere coincidence or luck. But coincidence and luck are pervasive in any area of life.

Suppose no one had *any* ability to make accurate market recommendations. Even then, if there are tens of thousands of Market-Beaters making recommendations (and there are), at any given moment the rules of probability alone dictate that some of them will be on amazing winning streaks.

If just 4,000 people were flipping coins over and over, at least one of them would flip heads 10 times in a row. Amazing! But would you bet your life savings on him to flip heads the next time?

Of course, a coin-flipping contest involves pure luck, and an investment advisor may have other resources—such as his experience, talent, and knowledge. But since Lady Luck will bring us a number of big winners each year, you can't know which winners are her children and which made it on their own.

Luck (good or bad) is simply what results from circumstances you can't control or know in advance. And since no advisor can control the market or be aware of everything that will contribute to tomorrow's events, luck will have to play a part in his future.

## Why the Lesson Works

Why did I say (on page 17) that someone's good record is likely to fall apart when you start acting on his advice?

Because you don't act on the advice of someone you never heard of. And you hear of him only after—and because—he has made several profitable recommendations in a row.

After he compiles a winning streak (for whatever reason), he becomes known and celebrated. But by then his lucky streak probably has run its course, and he's ready to begin losing—perhaps at the very time you start acting on his advice.

That's why the lesson others have learned the hard way is neither mysterious nor whimsical:

> *The investment expert with the perfect record up to now will lose his touch as soon as you start acting on his advice.*

## Helpers, Not Market-Beaters

Investment advisors acting as Helpers can be very useful—helping you set up a portfolio and translating some of the more mysterious areas of investing for you.

But when they put on their Market-Beater hats, promising to provide a better return than the market is offering to everyone else, watch out.

**RULE #6**

# Don't Expect
# a Trading System to Make
# You Rich

If someone were to tell you he'd discovered a foolproof way of handicapping horse races, picking lottery numbers, or beating the football pools, you might nod your head—but you'd be wondering how to remove yourself from the conversation.

But suppose he told you the system had already worked five times in a row—and he'd made several hundred dollars from it?

You might not be able to articulate your reasons, but probably you still wouldn't want to start using his system. You'd know the story was too good to be true—that the real world doesn't provide systems that make it easy to beat the odds.

You've probably never regretted turning your back on such a scheme. And if you ever checked back later, I imagine you found that the system had stopped working—and that the person using it had lost a good deal of money before giving up on it.

Or perhaps none of this sounds familiar to you. You can't recall ever being offered a sure-fire gambling system.

But you almost certainly have received such offers if you've read much about investments. The investment world is full of sure-fire ways to beat the markets. In fact, you can be offered more hot trading systems in a week than you'll come across in a lifetime at the race track.

Trading systems are programs, indicators, or other automatic signals that tell you explicitly when to buy and when to sell—without your having to make any decisions on your own.

For some of these systems, a moving average of investment prices generates the buy and sell signals. Others use ratios or differences between investment prices, some other statistical indicator, or even a numerical combination of several indicators.

Every trading system comes with the assurance that it's been tested scientifically—guaranteeing that you'll beat the market. And, needless to say, it will already have a fabulous track record—having signaled over and over where you should have put your money.

But somehow the systems never come through when your money is on the line. So please remember the first principle of trading systems:

*The system that has worked perfectly up to now will go sour when you stake your money on it.*

The system's apparent success so far may be due entirely to coincidence or good luck. Unless you can point to a very good reason the system should work, based upon the way real human beings behave, there's no reason to expect its success to continue.

Just as some advisors selectively reconstruct their track records, so do many proponents of trading systems. The true record may not be as good as the one you're shown.

And, of course, you won't hear today about the systems

that were infallible yesterday—and then failed. In fact, in many cases today's "perfect" trading system is a revised version of a system that had worked well for a while, but then stumbled and had to be redesigned.

## Where Trading Systems Come From

Trading systems generally arise from one of two sources.

The first source is a common-sense observation about human behavior—which someone then tries to transform into a quantifiable, mechanical system.

For example, Contrary Opinion is a theory that says, among other things, that an investment is likely to be near its peak when everyone seems to know how good its prospects are.

The idea makes some sense. If everyone already knows something is a good investment, most people who are likely to buy it probably already have done so—leaving very few investors to buy it and push its price still higher.

In such a case, you should be skeptical about its prospects as a speculation. But that doesn't mean we know precisely when or at what price the investment will peak. You know only that there doesn't *seem* to be room for the price to go much higher.

But people who devise trading systems aren't satisfied with anything so indefinite. They devise indicators to measure the precise degree of bullishness and bearishness surrounding a specific investment—and then construct formulas that provide specific signals for buying and selling.

This is similar to taking an obvious truth—such as that attendance at sporting events is generally smaller on rainy days than on sunny days—and constructing a formula that supposedly translates the number of inches of rainfall into an exact forecast of the attendance.

Human activity, human values, and human intentions can't be measured and quantified as though you were weighing a sack of apples or measuring the length of a twig. What you know about the way people act and the way markets seem to work is important, and this can provide general rules to guide you. But there's no way to translate any truism—no matter how clearly true—into a mathematical formula that can tell you accurately when to buy or sell.

A second source of trading systems is "data mining." An individual uses a computer to search through investment history—looking to see how various economic or market indicators match up with changes in investment prices. He hopes to find that some economic or market event always leads to a particular result for an investment.

If he looks hard enough, he's bound to find some amazing correlations. After all, there are trillions of possible combinations of events. If he checks enough data, he could even find that, say, every time the temperature topped 90° for ten days in a row, stock prices changed direction a week later. Or, more relevantly, that whenever the volume of shares traded exceeded some figure ten days in a row, the stock market changed direction.

Whatever he finds, he'll treat as a law of nature. After all, if it happened four or five times in a row, that's too often to be coincidence, isn't it?

No, it isn't. Whatever the reason for the past correlation (if there *was* a reason), the future is a different story. Transforming a curiosity of history into a trading system assumes that the same conditions will prevail in the future. But since the exact same conditions *won't* prevail (the participants won't be the same and all participants will be working with different knowledge from what they had in the past), the future can't duplicate the past.

Trading systems are based on the unstated assumption that the world doesn't change. But the world is in constant change—as desires change, demand changes, and supplies change. Otherwise there would be no price movements for investors to try to profit from. And these changes mean that, even if B followed A five times in the past, there's no assurance A will lead to B in the future.

History doesn't flow from a Xerox machine. And human beings aren't automatons who will act in the future as they did in the past. History never repeats itself—not literally, nor even figuratively—because people learn from experience, they change, and they change events.

Otherwise we'd still be trying to figure out how to cross the river Jordan.

## Successes and Failures

Of course, any trading system brought to your attention will have a fabulous record of success; otherwise, no one would bother telling you about it. But no matter how a system worked before, the future will unfold in its own way—oblivious to what seems predestined to us.

We have no way to know whether a trading system's past success was pure coincidence (very likely) or based on some real-world relationship (very rare). But even if it were the latter, those relationships change as people change, institutions change, procedures change, and the world changes.

And since you don't hear about a trading system until it has run up a good track record (for whatever reason), you are fair game for the first principle of trading systems:

> *The system that has worked perfectly up to now will go sour when you stake your money on it.*

**RULE #7**

# Invest Only
# on a Cash Basis

When someone goes completely broke, it's almost always because he was operating with borrowed money—even someone who was quite rich.

Using borrowed money increases the size of a purchase—and thus increases the potential profit from a speculation or a business deal. If the investment does well, you earn profits not only on the money you invested, but also on the money you borrowed. By borrowing enough to double your purchase, you approximately double the profit you'll earn if the investment does well.

But you also double the loss if the investment does poorly.[1]

When you see a "golden opportunity," it's natural to get carried away with how much you'll make if everything goes well. So borrowing money can seem like a smart way to exploit the opportunity.

But no investment is foolproof. Its outcome will depend on far more factors than you or anyone else can identify. People you've never heard of will make decisions, to buy or sell, that will push your investment toward success or failure. Bor-

---

[1] Because you have to pay interest on the borrowed money, your actual profit will be a bit less than double what it would have been without borrowing, or your loss will be a bit more than double that of a cash investment.

rowed money can just as easily enlarge your loss as increase your profit.

## Think and Go Broke

From time to time, you hear about a billionaire going broke. And the news can be disheartening.

After all, if such a person—with access to the most expensive advice in the world—can lose everything, it's easy to believe your chances of staying afloat are pretty slim.

But the billionaire didn't fail because he received a bad forecast, lacked access to the right kind of information, picked the wrong person to manage his money, or chose a poor investment. Any of those things might hurt, but what sends a billionaire to the poorhouse is his rejection of common sense.

Almost always the immediate problem is borrowed money. For example, a mega-millionaire decides to build an office complex. He may put up many millions of his own dollars, but then he'll borrow an amount five to ten times greater than that.

The investment does poorly—losing perhaps a third of its original cost. The value of the property sinks below the size of the loan, which must be repaid. There isn't enough left in the business to cover it. The mega-millionaire has to reach into his personal wealth to make up the difference between the money he borrowed and the remaining value of the business— and he's wiped out.

Had he exercised the same prudence he probably applies in other areas of his life, he wouldn't have gone overboard betting borrowed money on the outlook for a specific speculation.

On a smaller scale, similar problems can occur when an investor buys what looks like a high-potential stock or commodity—and buys even more by borrowing money from the broker (margin buying). High-potential speculations also can be high-potential losers. The price can drop so suddenly that the loss is greater than the amount invested—requiring that the investor cough up additional money, perhaps a lot of money.

You can avoid this kind of fate. Investing on a cash basis doesn't insure you against loss. But it effectively eliminates the risk of losing everything, because investment prices rarely go to zero. And if you diversify—not just among stocks, but across investment markets—even a severe loss in one market can be offset, or even overshadowed, by profits in another.[2]

In your personal life, you know that debt can be dangerous—that it is better to earn interest than pay it, that it's easy to get in trouble once you start borrowing. The investment world is no different.

Handle your business and investment affairs on a cash basis, and it's virtually impossible to lose everything—no matter what might happen in the world—especially if you follow the other rules in this book.

---

[2] Employing diversification profitably is covered by Rule #11.

# Make Your
# Own Decisions

Many individuals have lost their fortunes because they gave someone (usually a financial advisor or attorney) the authority to make their decisions and handle their money.

The advisor may have taken too many chances, been dishonest, or simply been incompetent. Even when there is no wrongdoing, no advisor can be expected to treat your wealth with the same respect you give to it.

You don't need a money manager. Investing is complicated and difficult only if you're trying to speculate and beat the market. To keep what you have requires only a simple understanding of the basics of investing. You can set up a worry-proof portfolio for yourself in one day—and thereafter you need only one day a year to monitor it.

Setting up such a portfolio for yourself is safer than turning your decisions over to anyone—even to the smartest person in the world.

*Above all,* never give anyone signature authority over money that's precious to you. If you ever put money into an account for someone else to manage, it must be money you can afford to lose—and you must have written verification that you are liable for no more than the money you've already given to the manager.[1]

---

[1] Signature authority means giving someone the legal authority to make financial transactions on your behalf without having your signature on each transaction.

You have no way of knowing what a money manager may be prompted to do someday by circumstances you know nothing about—his own financial problems, the pressure to keep his performance record competitive, or even problems that aren't related to his work but that impair his decision-making.

Once you accept that all the decisions are yours to make, you can entertain anyone's advice—through newsletters, personal consultations, books, whatever. These sources may help you clarify your own thinking, your own goals, and your own strategy.

But if you expect someone to make the right decisions for you, you're in trouble. No one (not even I) will ever treat your money with the same care you will.

# Do Only What
# You Understand

Don't ever undertake an investment, a speculation, or an investment program that you don't understand.

If you do, you later may discover risks you hadn't been aware of—or the risks may find you. You might even discover that your losses are greater than the amount you thought you were investing.

It doesn't matter whether your favorite investment advisor, your best friend, or your brother-in-law understands the investment perfectly. It isn't his money. He may be able to handle risks you can't, or he may know how to exit the investment at the right time. Because he isn't you, his understanding and judgment won't protect you.

It's better to leave your money in Treasury bills or a bank savings account than to sail into waters that for you are uncharted—where you don't even know what the potential losses might be.

Someday you might understand a particular investment well enough to know whether it's right for you. But until you do, it's better to leave it alone.

No complicated investment is essential for safety and security. As we'll see, you can construct a simple portfolio on your own that will take care of you in any economic environment. You don't have to rely on something you don't understand.

## Spread the Risk

Every investment has its time in the sun—and its moment of shame.

- Precious metals ruled the roost in the 1970s, while stocks and bonds were in disgrace.

- Gold and silver became the losers of the 1980s, while stocks and bonds multiplied their value.

- Real estate was a big winner in the 1970s, but lost its luster when the tax rules changed in 1986.

No one investment is good for all times. Even U.S. Treasury bills can lose real value during times of inflation.

We've seen, too, that you can't rely on any institution to protect your wealth for you. Old-line banks have failed, pension funds have come under a cloud of suspicion, and scandals—both real and imagined—are common on Wall Street. The company you depend on to keep your wealth may no longer be there when you're ready to withdraw your life savings.

Nor can you depend on any advisor to steer you safely from one investment to another as the economic winds change. Despite all the amazing track records you read about, no one can guarantee that he'll be right when your money is on the line.

When you depend upon one investment, one institution, or one person to see you through, you must constantly worry that your one source of security might fail.

But when you diversify across investments and institutions—and keep things simple enough to manage yourself—you can relax, knowing that no one event can do you in.

**RULE #11**

# Build a Bulletproof
# Portfolio for Protection

For the money you're counting on to take care of you for the
rest of your life, set up a simple, balanced, diversified portfolio.[1]

The portfolio should assure that your wealth will survive
any event—including events that would be devastating to any
one investment. In other words, this portfolio should protect
you *no matter what the future brings*.

It isn't difficult or complicated to build a bulletproof portfolio. You can achieve a great deal of protection with a surprisingly simple mix of investments.

The three absolute requirements for such a portfolio are:

**1. Safety:** It should protect you against every possible
economic future. You should profit during times of normal prosperity, but you also should be safe (and perhaps
even profit) during bad times—inflation, recession, or
even depression.

**2. Stability:** Whatever economic climate arrives, the
portfolio's performance should be so steady that you
won't wonder whether the portfolio needs to be changed.
Even in the worst possible circumstances, the portfolio's

---

[1] A portfolio is a collection of investments you hold.

value should drop no more than slightly—so that you won't panic and abandon it. This stability also permits you to turn your attention away from your investments, confident that your portfolio will protect you in any circumstance.

**3. Simplicity:** The portfolio should be so easy to maintain, and require so little of your time, that you'll never be tempted to look for something that seems simpler, but is less safe.

I call such a portfolio the Permanent Portfolio, because once you set it up, you never need to reconsider the investment mix—even if your outlook for the future changes. You leave it alone—to hold the same investments, in the same proportions, *permanently*. You don't change the proportions as you, your friends, or investment gurus change their minds about the future.

## Four Investments Cover
## All the Possibilities

How can you cover yourself against all possible futures?

Although there are millions of possibilities for the future, you don't have to worry about all of them individually. Most of what happens in the economy and the investment markets are just symptoms of the broad, underlying movements.

Your portfolio needs to respond well only to those broad movements. And they fit into four general categories:

1. *Prosperity:* A period during which living standards are rising, the economy is growing, business is thriving, interest rates usually are falling, and unemployment is declining.

2. *Inflation:* A period when consumer prices generally are rising. They might be rising moderately (an inflation rate of 6% or so), rapidly (10% to 20% or so, as in the late 1970s), or at a runaway rate (25% or more).

3. *Tight money or recession:* A period during which the growth of the supply of money in circulation slows down. This leaves people with less cash than they expected to have, and usually leads to a recession—a period of poor economic conditions.

4. *Deflation:* The opposite of inflation. Consumer prices decline and the purchasing power value of money grows. In the past, deflation has sometimes triggered a depression—a prolonged period of very bad economic conditions, as in the 1930s.

Investment prices can be affected by what happens outside the financial system—wars, changes in government policies, new tax rules, civil turmoil, and other matters. But these events have a lasting effect on investments only if they push the economy from one to another of the four environments I've just described.

The four economic categories are all-inclusive. At any time, one of them will predominate. So if you're protected in these four situations, you're protected in all situations.

## Investments Tied to the Economy

To be protected in all circumstances, each economic environment must have at least one investment in the Permanent Portfolio that responds well to it. Fortunately, there are simple investments that can do that.

*Prosperity* produces an upward market in stocks. And as prosperity causes interest rates to fall, long-term bonds go up in price.[2]

*Inflation* weakens faith in the U.S. dollar—the world's most popular money. As a result, many investors around the world reduce their dollar holdings and replace them with the world's second most popular form of money: gold. Once U.S. inflation becomes more than a minor irritant (that is, once inflation reaches 6% or so), gold usually starts moving upward—and when the inflation rate gets into double digits, gold's rise accelerates.

*Deflation* reduces the prices of most consumer goods and investments. As dollars become more valuable, interest rates fall dramatically. And as interest rates fall, bond prices go up. During the depression of the 1930s, for example, the interest yield on U.S. Treasury bonds fell to 2%. A drop to 2% from, say, 6% would cause long-term bonds to double in price.

*Tight money* is usually characterized by rising interest rates, which are bad for most investments. The only attractive investment during a recession is cash. And your cash holdings may not completely offset the losses that tight money may inflict on the rest of your portfolio.

[2] Bond prices automatically rise as interest rates fall, and bond prices fall as interest rates rise—that is, bonds and interest rates move in opposite directions. A stockbroker can provide literature that explains how the bond market works.

But tight money is by nature a temporary condition. Unlike prosperity, inflation, or depression, it can't go on indefinitely. Either the economy adjusts to the new level of money and returns to prosperity, or the supply of money changes—leading to inflation or a full-scale deflation.

## Four Investments Cover All

Thus four investments provide coverage for all four economic environments:

*Stocks* take advantage of prosperity. They tend to do poorly during periods of inflation, deflation, and tight money, but over time those periods don't undo the gains that stocks achieve during periods of prosperity.

*Bonds* also take advantage of prosperity. In addition, they profit when interest rates collapse during a deflation. You should expect bonds to do poorly during times of inflation and tight money.

*Gold* not only does well during times of intense inflation, it does *very* well. In the 1970s, gold rose twenty times over as the inflation rate soared to its peak of 15% in 1980. Gold generally does poorly during times of prosperity, tight money, and deflation.

*Cash* is most profitable during a period of tight money. Not only is it a liquid asset that can give you purchasing power when your income and investments might be ailing, but the rise in interest rates increases the return on your dollars. Cash also becomes more valuable during a deflation as prices fall. Cash is essentially neutral during a time of prosperity, and it is a loser during times of inflation.

## Neutrality?

It might seem that a Permanent Portfolio containing these four contradictory investments would be neutralized: As one element rose, another would fall—and nothing would be gained.

On a day-to-day basis, that can be true. But over broad periods of time, the winning investments add more value to the portfolio than the losing investments take away.

For example, during 1973–77, stocks generally lost about 20%, but gold rose by 153%. During 1981–86, gold fell 34%, while stocks rose 80%. During these periods, stocks and gold didn't cancel each other out; the winner had a bigger impact on the overall outcome than the loser did. The portfolio continued to appreciate in value—no matter what the climate.

The graph on page 44 shows the results for the Permanent Portfolio for the 29 years from January 1970 through December 1998. The portfolio provided an average gain of 9.9% per year, which was 4.5% per year above inflation.

The period covered by the graph encompasses most of the economic environments your portfolio might have to face. The 1970s were plagued with inflation. Prosperity reigned during much of the 1980s and 1990s. And there were recessions in 1970, 1973–75, 1980, 1981–82, and 1990–92. The only economic climate not included in the period was an outright deflation, such as America suffered during the early 1930s.[3]

---

[3] I made the last major refinement to the Permanent Portfolio concept in 1987—a revision that made the portfolio simpler to set up and maintain. The graph uses the actual results for the portfolio since December 31, 1987, together with a hypothetical representation of how the same portfolio would have performed before then.

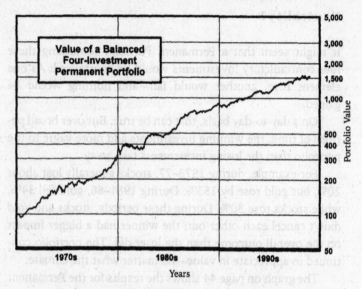

**Value of a Balanced Four-Investment Permanent Portfolio**

1970s        1980s        1990s

Years

How did the portfolio measure up to the three standards I have set for a portfolio?

**1. *Safety:*** The portfolio continued growing through every economic environment it faced. It even gained value (in real, after-inflation terms) during the inflationary 1970s. With such a portfolio, you know you're safe no matter what may come.

**2. *Stability:*** A striking feature of the graph is the Permanent Portfolio's stability. It achieved steady growth— sheltering its owner from the extremes that most investors faced. In 29 years the portfolio lost value in only three years—6.2% in 1981, 0.7% in 1990, and 2.4% in 1994. And those were years in which most investments lost value. In particular, 1981 was a terrible year for *every* major investment—stocks, bonds, foreign currencies, commodities, gold, and silver—and most investors took a terrible beating that year. Each of the Permanent Portfolio's three losing years was followed by rapid gains that overshadowed the small losses.

On October 19, 1987, when the Dow Jones Industrial Average fell 22.6% in one day, the 4-investment Permanent Portfolio lost only 4.3% of its value. Despite the stock market crash, the portfolio finished 1987 with a gain of 5.3% for the year.

**3. *Simplicity:*** For most investors, this portfolio requires no more than one short day to set up. Thereafter, you need to monitor it *only once a year*—merely to determine whether changes in investment prices have unbalanced the portfolio's mix of investments.

The portfolio's gains were achieved without foreseeing the future, without dependence upon a guru or system to move with split-second timing from one investment to another—in fact with no switching among investments at all.

## Composition of the Portfolio

The portfolio's effectiveness depends upon the percentage of your capital you assign to each of the four investments.

No magic formula can tell you which distribution of investments will produce the best return over the next decade. And any attempt to be clever in assigning portions to the investments probably will do more harm than good. I prefer the simplicity of allocating 25% to each of the four investments.

Here, for example, is the allocation to the investments with three possible amounts of starting capital:[4]

| STARTING CAPITAL | $10,000 | $50,000 | $100,000 |
|---|---|---|---|
| Stocks | $2,500 | $12,500 | $25,000 |
| Bonds | 2,500 | 12,500 | 25,000 |
| Gold | 2,500 | 12,500 | 25,000 |
| Cash | 2,500 | 12,500 | 25,000 |

Each investment must have a substantial share, because the time will come when it is asked to carry the entire portfolio. And each investment will do poorly at times, so no investment should have too large a share.

The portfolio's safety is assured by the contrasting qualities of the four investments—which ensure that any event that damages one investment should be good for one or more of the others. And no investment, even at its worst, can devastate the portfolio—no matter what surprises lurk around the corner—because no investment has more than 25% of your capital.

## Annual Checkup and Rebalancing

Once established, you can pretty much forget about the Permanent Portfolio if you want to. The only maintenance required is to check the portfolio's makeup once a year.

[4] As explained on page 113, you can start a Permanent Portfolio with as little as $1,000.

As investment prices change during the year, one or more of the investments will grow to become worth more than 25% of the portfolio's total value. And one or more investments will be worth less than 25% of the new total value.

If any of the four investments has become worth less than 15%, or more than 35%, of the portfolio's overall value, you need to restore the original percentages. Otherwise, you'll be relying too much on the most successful investment to continue being successful, and you'll be leaving some other investment with too small a share to carry the portfolio when its time comes to pull the load.

To rebalance the portfolio to its original percentages, just sell enough of the leading investments to reduce each to 25% of the total value. Use the proceeds from those sales to buy more of the investments that have fallen under 25%.

This will "lock in" some of the profits earned by the winners, and make sure that the losers are in position to help when their time comes to shine.

When you make your once-a-year check of the portfolio's value, if all four investments are within the 15–35% range, no rebalancing is necessary.

During the year, if you happen to notice that there's been a big change in investment prices, you may want to check the values of the investments. Again, if any investment has strayed outside the 15–35% range, go ahead and rebalance the entire portfolio.

## Safety, Stability, Simplicity

The test of a Permanent Portfolio is whether it provides peace of mind.

A Permanent Portfolio should let you watch the evening news or read investment publications in total serenity. No actual or threatened event should trouble you, because you'll know that your portfolio is protected against it.

If someone warns about the "alarming parallels" between the current decade and the 1920s, you shouldn't wonder whether you need to sell all your stocks. You'll know that your Permanent Portfolio will take care of you—even if next year turns out to be 1929 revisited. The deflation that could devastate stocks would push interest rates downward and bring big profits for your bonds.

When someone claims the inflation rate is headed back to 15%, you shouldn't wonder whether to dump all your bonds. You'll know that the gain in your Permanent Portfolio's gold would far outweigh any losses on the bonds.

When someone announces that a new debt crisis is on the way, or that a bull market is about to begin in stocks, bonds, or gold, you won't feel pressured to decide whether he's right. You'll know that the Permanent Portfolio will respond favorably to any eventuality.

I can't list every potential event. So if you become concerned by any possibility, reread this chapter and you should be reassured that there's an investment in your Permanent Portfolio that will cover you if the worst should occur.

Whatever the potential crisis or opportunity, your Permanent Portfolio should already be taking care of you.

The portfolio can't guarantee a profit every year; no portfolio can. It won't outperform the hotshot advisor in his best year. And it won't outperform the best investment of the year.

But it can give you the confidence that no crisis will destroy you, the assurance that your savings are secure and growing in all circumstances, and the knowledge that you're no longer vulnerable to the mistakes in judgment that you or the best advisor could so easily make.

It's all as it should be—safe and simple.

**RULE #12**

# Speculate Only with Money
# You Can Afford to Lose

Despite my efforts to discourage you from betting on forecasts, trading systems, or gurus, I won't blame you for still wanting to hit it big. I realize that if you passed up an opportunity, you might wonder for the rest of your life whether you would have made a fortune—large or small.

Well, I have good news for you. I'm not asking you to give up the hope of making big money in the investment markets.

I have nothing against your speculating. My single admonition is:

*Speculate only with money you can afford to lose.*

Understand, too, that I'm not saying you *should* speculate. Most people have no interest in it. And although someone may tell you today's conditions require you to be adventurous, you don't need anything more than a balanced Permanent Portfolio.

But if you do want to try to beat the markets, set aside a separate sum of money with which you can speculate to your heart's content. Just make sure that it's no more than you can afford to lose.

I call this sum of money a Variable Portfolio, because its investments vary as your outlook for the future changes.

The Permanent Portfolio is for the money that's precious

to you—the capital you're counting on for retirement or to pass on to your heirs. I believe you should never take chances with that capital—never use a penny of it to bet on someone's forecast or to use market timing of any kind.

But the Variable Portfolio (if you want to have one) is funded with money you've already decided you can afford to lose. Thus you can use it to try to build a big fortune or just to have fun—taking whatever chances you want, knowing that the worst possible loss won't devastate you.

## Uses for the Variable Portfolio

When you think stocks are in a bull market, you might put the Variable Portfolio wholly into stocks. If you see tough times coming, you might put it into bonds or gold or foreign currencies. And when you have no strong expectations, you might leave the entire Variable Portfolio in cash.

Or there might be times when the Variable Portfolio is partly in one thing, partly in another—or partly invested and partly in cash. Any combination is okay.

In fact, any trading method is acceptable; any forecast can be used. Follow an appealing system, your intuition, your favorite advisor, a preferred astrologer, or any guiding light you choose.

You also can turn the Variable Portfolio over to a money manager to handle for you. So long as you have written assurance that you aren't liable for any more money than you've given the money manager, and so long as you aren't using Permanent Portfolio money, there's nothing wrong with trusting someone to try to make a fortune for you.

Segregating assets into a separate Variable Portfolio frees your hand. Because you know you aren't risking wealth that's precious to you, you're free to act on any judgment you believe will make money for you.

Once again, there's nothing wrong with speculating. Just do it with a second portfolio, so there's no chance you'll risk capital that's precious to you.

Have some excitement. Go for the brass ring. Do something you can brag about—*but only with money you can afford to lose.*

# Keep Some Assets
# Outside Your Own Country

For complete safety, don't allow everything you own to be within the reach of your government. If you keep some assets in a different country, you'll be less vulnerable, and you'll feel less vulnerable. You won't have to worry so much about what your government might do next.[1]

The Permanent Portfolio will be safe enough to walk away from and forget about completely only if it allows for more than just the problems and hazards that are obvious today. It will have to allow for all the unforeseeable events of the next 5, 10, 15, or 20 years.

Keeping some investments abroad provides safe and easy protection against surprises that might happen anywhere—confiscation of gold holdings by the government, exchange controls, civil disorder, even war.

Here are some of the benefits of overseas holdings:

1. You'll have the time and opportunity to respond to any extraordinary policies adopted by your own government. No one knows how the people elected in the coming years might choose to solve the economic problems the country will face. It might

---

[1] This applies no matter where you live.

strike them that the quick and easy solution is to take your property—as has happened so often already.

2. Your assets will be safe even if war, civil disorder, a weakening of law enforcement, or a physical catastrophe should disrupt record-keeping in your own country.

3. You'll have some wealth out of reach of the litigation sharks in your society.

4. Your entire estate will no longer be vulnerable to economic, political, or legal setbacks in your own country.

These hazards may seem remote. And they are—in the sense that I have no reason to expect them to touch you now. But they are real hazards, and now and then you feel that reality—when a politician urges something especially dangerous or foolish, or it's revealed that the tax collectors are acting in a particularly heavy-handed way, or an international conflict threatens to erupt into something big.

Someday a remote hazard will grow into an immediate threat. Geographic diversification is a necessary part of making sure the Permanent Portfolio can handle whatever hazard materializes.

Keeping some of your holdings overseas may seem at first to be the opposite of simplicity in your investment program. But opening and maintaining a foreign bank account requires little effort. It is much like having an account with an American bank or brokerage firm that you never visit in person.

Once you open the account by mail, it requires practically no monitoring.[2]

Then you'll probably begin to develop a more relaxed attitude about the future. When some politician promises to fight the trade deficit or some other problem by building a wall around your country with foreign exchange controls, you shouldn't get the feeling that you're trapped. You'll know that you already have gold or some other asset sitting outside the reach of your government.

[2] Information on some foreign banks is provided on page 163.

# Take Advantage of Tax-Reduction Plans

Income taxes make you devote from a third to a half of your working life to the government's benefit, rather than your own. If you didn't have to pay income tax, it's not hard to imagine what you could do for yourself, your family, your church, and your favorite charity.[1]

Fortunately, there are some things you can do to minimize your tax bill. They aren't flashy, daring, or innovative. They also aren't even dangerous or hard to understand.

I encourage you to take advantage of the simple tax-reduction strategies available—and to shun those that are too complicated for you to evaluate.

## Types of Tax-Reduction

You can reduce taxes on your investments in two ways.

The first is to be able to deduct the purchase of an investment from your taxable income. Normally, if you want to make $5,000 worth of investments, you have to earn, say, $7,000—paying $2,000 of that in income tax, leaving $5,000 net to invest. It would be better if you could avoid tax on the

---

[1] According to the U.S. Census Bureau, as of 1997 all kinds of taxes—direct and indirect, federal, state, and local—eat up 47% of the national income.

money to be invested—so that you had to earn only $5,000 to be able to invest $5,000.

The second way is to avoid taxes on the income your investments produce—the dividends paid by stocks, the interest earned by bonds and money market funds, and possibly even the profits earned by stocks, bonds, or gold. When your full investment income and profits can be reinvested and compounded, without being diminished by taxes, your nest egg will grow much, much faster.

This second way is illustrated in the graph below, showing the difference between two investment accounts. For simplicity, each starts at $1,000 and earns 5% per year. The sheltered account pays no taxes on the 5%; the non-sheltered account has one quarter of the 5% diverted to taxes each year—so

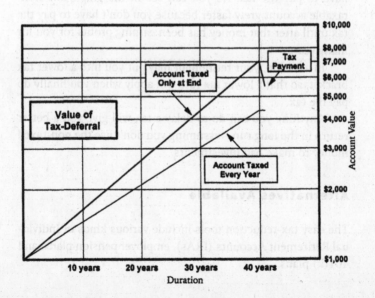

there's less money upon which to earn next year's 5%. What may seem like a small difference in net yearly earnings compounds into a 61% difference at the end of your working career.

Even if, at the end of your career, you had to pay a 25% tax on all the gains accumulated over the 40 years (as shown in the graph), you'd still come out 27% ahead of the account that paid taxes year by year.

## Tax Deferral

This is *tax deferral*—the basic method for reducing the tax burden on your investment program.

With tax deferral, the money you don't pay in taxes today can work to produce more earnings every year until you finally have to pay the tax. As you can see in the graph, the non-taxable account grew faster because you don't have to pay the tax until after that money has been earning profits for you for many years.

In addition, your retirement may put you into a lower tax bracket, so that a lower tax rate will apply when you finally do pay the tax.

Anything you can do to delay a tax will give you a better return in the long run—assuming you don't use the non-taxed money to make bad investments.

## Alternatives Available

The easy tax-reduction tools include various kinds of Individual Retirement Accounts (IRAs), employer pension plans, and 401(k) plans.

With most of them, each year you can divert a portion of your working income to investments in a pension plan. You pay no income tax on the earnings you put into the pension plan. And you pay no tax on the income and profits that accumulate within the pension plan. When you retire, you pay tax on the money as you withdraw it from the plan. The long-term advantage is considerable, but there's a limit to how much of your income you can legally divert each year to the pension plan.

Other alternatives require that you pay tax on the money you earn and put into the pension plan, but then allow you to accumulate investment income and profits tax-free. Here, too, there are limits on how much you can put into the plan each year, even though you're paying taxes on the money before you invest it.

You can have more than one pension plan. And it's useful to take advantage of every alternative open to you.

## How to Set Up Pension Plans

Setting up a pension plan is relatively easy in most cases. If it's a company pension plan, your employer will take care of it for you.

For other plans, almost any bank, mutual fund, or stockbroker can arrange a plan for you—as long as you use its investments. Thus a mutual fund will set up an IRA, for example, that invests exclusively in that fund. Since you can have more than one IRA (provided you don't put more money into all of them together than the legal limits permit), you can have IRAs with several funds.

Many stockbrokers offer pension plans with lengthy menus of investments—including stocks, bonds, Treasury bills, and maybe even gold coins. You can choose from among those investments and switch from one to another. This makes it easy to rebalance your portfolio whenever you need to get it back to its original percentages.[2]

Anyone offering an IRA or other pension plan should have literature available that explains the plan.

It isn't possible to set up a tax-advantaged pension plan outside the United States.

For privacy and liquidity, some money should be kept outside of pension plans. But after satisfying those needs, you probably have every reason to use pension plans as much as possible.

## Getting More Information

If you work for a large company, it may have an "employee benefits" office or other department that can help you understand the alternatives available to you. If not, talk to a banker or stockbroker.

In any case, remember that when all the talking is done, you must make the decisions. No one can choose for you.

Remember, too, that financial professionals you talk with won't look at investing in the way I've presented in this book. Most counselors will suggest that you invest entirely in stocks, or they will tell you which investments they expect to do es-

[2] Adjustments are explained on pages 46–47.

pecially well. They won't suggest the balanced portfolio I've recommended in this book.

But these people still can help you by letting you know which tax-deferral plans you're qualified to use.

**RULE #15**

## Ask the Right Questions

Very often, investors buy the wrong investments for their needs because they ask the wrong questions.

Here are five questions investors frequently ask that cloud the issues and lead to confusion—together with questions that will help you get the information you really need.

### Risk

#### 1. "Is there any risk?"

Of course there is risk. No investment is risk-free. Risk is simply the possibility that the investment won't do as well as expected.

What you want to know is:

- In what economic circumstances is the investment's price likely to go down?

- Are other investments in your portfolio likely to take up the slack by gaining in those same circumstances?

- What is the most you can lose on the investment? (Usually, every penny you put it into it.)

## Safety

### 2. "Is this investment safe?"

What does *safe* mean?

That the price can't go down? Bank accounts don't fall in price so long as the bank stays in business, but they can lose real value during inflationary periods.

No investment is perfectly safe. There isn't a single one that can't lose purchasing-power value in some circumstances.

What you want to know is:

- Under what circumstances could I lose a substantial share—20% or more—of my investment?

- Under what circumstances could my entire investment be lost?

- Would I have any residual liability—that is, can I lose even more than the cash I invest?

## Income and Capital Appreciation

### 3. "How much does the investment yield?"

Interest and dividends (an investment's yield) are two of the three ways you can gain from an investment. The third way is through a rise in the price of the investment.

All three ways give you money you can spend. But the first two ways are immediately taxable, while the third might not be taxable for many years.

Looking only for a high yield leads to two kinds of trouble. First, interest rates generally reflect an investment's risk.

A higher interest rate means there's a greater possibility the capital can be lost—through default or inflation. And a high dividend yield often means a stock isn't likely to appreciate in price—and may even mean the company is using some of its capital to pay dividends.

Second, chasing yields can blind you to other factors—and even may cause you to consume capital, rather than preserve it. Suppose, for example, that in 1970 you had put your capital into long-term Treasury bonds yielding 6%, with the thought that you would live off the high yield (for that era) while preserving the capital. But consumer prices doubled during the 1970s, cutting the purchasing power of the bond interest—and your standard of living—in half.

In addition, inflation drove current interest rates higher, so that bond prices steadily depreciated. Your capital was slipping away from you. Even if you held the bond to maturity, you got back dollars of much less value than those you had invested.

You may have thought you were "living off the income, not the capital," but by 1980 your capital had been cut by 20% in dollar value and 60% in actual purchasing power. And the income was buying only half the living standard expected of it.

Yield, by itself, is only a half-truth about the investment. What you also need to know is:

- Under what circumstances, if any, is the investment likely to appreciate?

- Under what circumstances, if any, is the investment likely to depreciate?

- In good circumstances for the investment, will the

overall return—yield plus capital appreciation—help your portfolio overcome losses in other investments?

If the investment is a mutual fund, you want the fund with the *lowest* yield—other things being equal. Any dividend paid by a mutual fund simply reduces the price of your shares by a comparable amount—so that the dividend is coming out of your own pocket. And even though you gain nothing from the dividend, it adds to the current year's taxable income—causing you to pay taxes on something that doesn't profit you.

## Takeover Candidate

**4. "Is this company a potential takeover candidate?"** (Or does it have some other fashionable characteristic?)

There is no information you can obtain about a company that isn't available to everyone else in the marketplace. Thus whatever is attractive about the company probably is already reflected in its stock price.

So if the company does what you're expecting, the price might go up a bit—as what was merely probable materializes into hard fact. But if the expected event fails to materialize, the price may drop a long way. So when you act on a takeover story (or some other widely held hope), you are risking a lot to gain a little—exactly opposite to what a speculation should be.

Large speculative profits are earned only by going against the crowd. The crowd isn't always wrong, but you can't make much betting with it—because you will buy at a price that's already high. By going against the crowd, you buy when an investment is out of favor and cheap; if it does succeed, there's a long way for it to go up.

So the most important factor in speculating is whether you expect something that most people don't expect. For example, the time to consider buying inflation hedges speculatively is when most people believe inflation is under control. The time to consider buying a particular company is when everyone knows what a dog it is—not when everyone talks about its great promise.

Unpopularity doesn't guarantee profits, but you'll never make a killing with a popular investment.

So don't ask or hope for significant information. Ask yourself instead:

- Do you interpret the widely known information in a different way from what most people believe?

## Technical Analysis

### 5. "Do the technical factors favor the investment now?"
That question really is a proxy for about 2,487 questions: Are the moving averages rising? Is investor sentiment bullish? Is that a head-and-shoulders formation I spy on the chart? Is its tail between its legs? And so on.

No matter how many times a given indicator has signaled correctly in the past, it has only an even chance of being right this time—just as you have an even chance of flipping a coin heads, no matter how many heads or tails have come up already.

Instead, ask yourself:

- Is there something on TV more interesting than these investment graphs?

## The Plan Dictates the Questions

Always define carefully what you are trying to achieve. You must have an investment plan.

Without a plan, you will be tossed and turned by all the conflicting ideas you read and hear—and you'll never ask the right questions.

With a plan, you'll have a basis for evaluating whatever you hear. You'll know to ask the questions that help you determine whether an investment furthers your plan.

**RULE #16**

# Enjoy Yourself with a
# Budget for Pleasure

Your wealth is of no value if you don't enjoy it.

It's easy to spend too much while you're earning money from your work—leaving you with too little for the future, when you may not want to work so hard.

That's not the only problem, though. You also can become afraid to spend money, for fear of impoverishing your future.

To enjoy some of your wealth while you're earning it, budget a sum of money that you can spend each year without concern for the consequences.

If you stay within that amount, you can feel free to blow the money on cars, trips, anything you want—without worry, because you'll know you aren't blowing your future.

# Whenever You're in Doubt,

# Err on the Side of Safety

At times you may feel forced to do something you don't understand. Or perhaps you believe you must evaluate an investment or plan even though the task calls for more sophistication than you possess. Or maybe someone insists that you make a decision now—and you feel you could lose your life savings if you jump the wrong way.

In any of these situations, what do you do?

No matter what else you may know, I hope you will hold on to this one rule:

*When in doubt about an investment decision, it is always better to err on the side of safety.*

If it turns out you're wrong, be wrong on the safe side. If you wind up losing something, let it be only an opportunity that was lost—not precious capital.

People rarely go broke playing it safe. But many go broke taking great risks or making investments they know too little about.

I don't mean you should never take risks. Such a policy isn't even possible. Every investment, every action—even inaction—involves risk of some kind. But whenever you aren't sure what to do, one answer is always correct: Play it safe.

If you're hesitating, it's because you don't yet know

enough about the investment or the problem to make a confident decision. That means you shouldn't take the plunge until you know more and you're sure you understand all the ramifications.

From time to time I have regretted that I failed to buy something I'd considered. But I've never been hurt by not buying.

Meanwhile, I've seen plenty of money lost by investors who were convinced they were facing the last chance to buy something. But there never really is a "last chance." Even if you miss out on a good speculation, other opportunities will follow.

It's harder to resist the stampede to an investment or a system when others seem to be raking in profits. But you don't know how well other people are really doing. Even if you're convinced that someone is doing very well, he may be doing it by taking risks that aren't right for you.

People don't go broke being too cautious, but they can be hurt badly by jumping into something they don't understand, haven't thought out, or can't afford.

If you pass up an opportunity to increase your fortune, there always will be another chance. But if you lose your life savings, you might not get a chance to recover.

> *When in doubt about an investment decision, it is always better to err on the side of safety.*

**Part II**

# More about the Rules

# More about Your Career
# and Your Wealth

You've probably heard of people who made a fortune investing. But in most cases they started with a sizeable stake—several hundred thousand dollars or more—from an inheritance or a previous career. Or they were full-time (60-hours-a-week) speculators. Or their riches came from advising investors, rather than by outperforming them in the markets. Or they had losses that were less publicized than their profits.

Even if you can find someone who has made big money speculating while holding a day job, realize that you've located a rare exception—not someone you can imitate.

In most cases, the siren song called "Get Rich Quick" is no more realistic than that of the con man on the street who tells you he has a way to double your money in two weeks.

## What You Can Achieve

By contrast, conservative investing can be very powerful because it focuses on realistic goals.

The power comes not only from the profits investments produce, but from the dynamics of compound interest—as your profits multiply through reinvestment.

Table 1 shows how well you can retire at age 65, based on

when you start saving and how much of your income you set aside for investing.

**T A B L E   1**

## Yearly Retirement Income As a Percentage of Your Final Year's Working Income

| STARTING AGE | Share of your working income you invest each year | | | | | |
|---|---|---|---|---|---|---|
| | 5% | 8% | 10% | 15% | 20% | 25% |
| 20 | 76% | 121% | 152% | 228% | 303% | 379% |
| 25 | 58% | 93% | 116% | 175% | 233% | 291% |
| 30 | 44% | 71% | 88% | 133% | 177% | 221% |
| 35 | 33% | 53% | 66% | 99% | 132% | 165% |
| 40 | 24% | 39% | 48% | 72% | 96% | 121% |
| 45 | 17% | 27% | 34% | 51% | 68% | 85% |
| 50 | 11% | 18% | 23% | 34% | 46% | 57% |
| 55 | 7% | 11% | 14% | 21% | 28% | 35% |
| 60 | 3% | 5% | 7% | 10% | 13% | 17% |

Each row is an age at which you might start saving, and each column is headed by the percentage of your working income that you put aside each year. The intersection of the row and column shows your annual retirement income as a percentage of your income in the final year that you work.

For example, if you begin investing at age 20 and set aside 10% of your annual income, your retirement income at age 65 will equal 74% of what you earned in your final working year.

If you earn $100,000 in your last working year, you'll have an annual retirement income of $74,000; if you earn $50,000 in your last working year, your annual retirement income will be $37,000.

The table assumes that—once retired—you'll live entirely off the income from your savings, without touching the capital, so that all the capital you've accumulated will remain in your estate.

As an alternative you could use the entire capital you've accumulated to buy a lifetime annuity—which means an insurance company will guarantee to pay you a specified income for so long as you live. In that case, you'll leave no capital for your heirs, but your annual income will be greater, as shown in Table 2.

That table shows the annual retirement income for a man, relying on a lifetime annuity.[1]

Of course, you can use a combination of the two approaches—buying a lifetime annuity at retirement with part of your capital and investing the rest. That way you can leave something for your heirs, but you also have a larger income than if you had conserved the entire capital.

Both tables assume that your working income rises by 5% each year.

The tables also assume that your investments earn the 9.9% per year earned by the Permanent Portfolio from 1970

[1] The annual income for a woman would be about 10% smaller, because insurance companies expect women to live longer. A joint and survivor annuity (wherein the death of one person allows the spouse or partner to continue receiving half the annual payment for the rest of his life) would produce an annual income about 9% less than that shown in Table 2.

TABLE 2

# Annual Retirement Income for a Man, As a Percentage of Your Final Year's Working Income If You Consume the Capital and Leave Nothing for Your Heirs

| STARTING AGE | Share of your working income you invest each year | | | | | |
|---|---|---|---|---|---|---|
| | 5% | 8% | 10% | 15% | 20% | 25% |
| 20 | 67% | 108% | 135% | 202% | 270% | 337% |
| 25 | 52% | 83% | 103% | 155% | 207% | 259% |
| 30 | 39% | 63% | 79% | 118% | 157% | 196% |
| 35 | 29% | 47% | 59% | 88% | 117% | 147% |
| 40 | 21% | 34% | 43% | 64% | 86% | 107% |
| 45 | 15% | 24% | 30% | 45% | 61% | 76% |
| 50 | 10% | 16% | 20% | 30% | 41% | 51% |
| 55 | 6% | 10% | 12% | 18% | 25% | 31% |
| 60 | 3% | 5% | 6% | 9% | 12% | 15% |

through 1998 (see page 44 for details). You may be hoping for more, but in an uncertain world your savings plan may not be safe or realistic if it needs to do better than that. Some years you may earn a good deal more, but you should allow for other years in which you barely break even or perhaps even lose a little.

## Retirement Needs

When examining the tables, remember that you aren't likely to need retirement income equal to 100% of what you make during your prime earning years. When you retire, you probably won't have the same financial needs you had earlier.

Your budget should no longer have such expenses as a mortgage payment, costs related to making a living (such as commuting costs or a particular wardrobe), the heavy expenses of raising a family, and many other costs you take for granted now. And you'll no longer be diverting part of your income to investments.

Also, the retirement income in the tables will be in addition to any pension funded by your employer. Nor do the tables allow for your employer's contributing anything to your own savings plan, which would increase your retirement income.

## Starting Early

Obviously, the earlier you start, the better you'll do. Not just because you'll save more, but because you'll have more years in which those savings are earning profits—and those profits in turn are compounding and earning additional profits.

If, in any given year, you can set aside more than your plan calls for, you can build up your retirement fund faster. Or you may want to put the excess into a separate investment fund for more immediate needs—such as your children's college education, accumulating the down payment for a home, or some other purchase.

# More about

# Protecting Your Wealth

The 1970s and 1980s brought us well-publicized stories of wealthy people who went broke or who lost most of what they had.

Businessman and politician John Connolly, renowned for his "insider's" ability to make money, one day found that he had to sell his most precious personal possessions at auction. To the best of my knowledge, years later he still hadn't been able to return to his previous lifestyle.

The Hunt Brothers inherited a fortune from their father's oil and food industry successes. But they lost hundreds of millions of dollars speculating in silver and oil in the early 1980s, and I've seen no news that they've been able to earn it back.

Actress Doris Day lost most of what she had when she discovered that her late husband had squandered their money on bad investments. She was able to recover part of what had been lost, but only through a long series of exhausting lawsuits.

Of course, these people aren't you. And it's easy to believe you won't make the same mistakes they did.

That's true. You probably won't. But that doesn't mean you won't make *any* mistakes. There are no books big enough to acquaint you with every possible hazard of trusting someone with your money, or betting with money you can't afford to lose, or risking too much on a sure thing.

It is far safer simply to assume that the wealth you need for your future is precious to you, that you won't be able to replace it if you lose it, and thus you can't take chances with it.

# More about Investing and Speculating

The goal of speculation is to make more than the investment markets are offering to other investors.

The premise for speculation is that you're more astute than most other investors—that you understand the market better, that you have information not available to other investors, that you can make better decisions, or that your interpretation of available information is especially perceptive.

The elements of speculation are timing, forecasting, trading systems, and selection. Any time you use any of these tactics you're speculating—even if someone tells you the risk is low.

The goal is understandable, but in most cases speculation is futile. Few investors beat the market for long. And those who *fail* to do so include investors who subscribe to newsletters, investors who have the counsel of high-priced and highly rated advisors, and investors who spend many hours at their computers working out the best systems and selections.

It seems so easy to beat the market. After all, you hear of so many people who have done it. And you hear of simple methods for selecting stocks or mutual funds—or of a seemingly sensible, foolproof trading system that tells you when to load up with stocks and when to dump them.

But even most professionals fail to outperform the return

the markets are offering everyone. If *they* can't do it—with all the research, the tools, and the attention they apply to the task—how likely is it that you'll succeed?

Speculation leads more often to losses than to gains—and even when you win, it is very difficult to beat the return the markets are offering to everyone else.

That doesn't mean you should never speculate. If you have a desire to speculate but then hold back, you may always wonder how well you would have done.

So I say once again: There's nothing wrong with speculating—*provided you do it only with money you can afford to lose.* But the wealth that's precious to you—the money you're counting on for retirement—should never be risked on a bet that you can outperform other investors.

**RULE #4**

# More about
# Fortune-Tellers and
# Forecasts

Investment forecasts can be exciting. But in other areas of our lives, we think of fortune-tellers as entertainers.

It can be fascinating when someone says a mysterious investment cycle is about to peak on a precise date next month. But how does this differ from the precise dates predicted for the end of the world—which come and go without your even breaking a fingernail?

It can be engrossing when someone says the graph of an investment's price shows a pattern that signals a major change in investment trends. But how does that differ from someone who sees the future in lines on the palm of your hand?

It's one thing to bet $5 on a horse because of a coincidental name—or to choose a vacation spot based on astrology advice in the daily paper. But should you bet on the mysterious insights of a crystal-gazer with the money it's taken you so long to save?

Don't do in the investment world what you wouldn't do elsewhere.

## Why Forecasts Are Unreliable

Reliable forecasts are impossible because the forecaster can't possibly be privy to enough information about the present to get a line on the future.

Next year's Dow Jones Averages will reflect billions of separate decisions—which themselves are the outgrowth of the desires, intentions, and actions of hundreds of millions of people of all kinds, not just investors.

Not even the world's biggest computer can read the minds of millions of people—and thus it can't obtain and analyze the data necessary to know the future. So investors try shortcuts.

They use fundamental analysis—such as guessing how politicians will try to manipulate interest rates, and what the manipulations will lead to. Or they apply technical analysis—such as watching the trends of particular indicators (like the volume of trading that accompanies price movements), thinking that the cause-and-effect pattern of yesterday will apply again tomorrow.

Almost any method works at first, because the analyzer chooses only the methods that *are* working. But no forecasting system holds up long enough to make you rich. And when it stops working, you lose money—because the one thing you certainly can't forecast is the occasion when a forecasting method will fail.

## Truth and Fiction

It can seem that some forecasters have good records. But that's because we know only what they choose to tell us—and they rarely advertise their failures.

Even a scorecard of all their hits and misses won't show us the original predictions, word-for-word in the original context. If it did, the statement "Last year I predicted the current rise in interest rates" might not seem so appropriate. If we could see the qualifications added to the forecast, the later reversals or moderation in the forecaster's advice, and other hedges and contradictions, it might be obvious that you wouldn't have made a single dollar off the advisor's "prediction."

Years ago I began accumulating file cabinets full of investment newsletters. When some writer boasted about last year's right-on-the-money prediction, I'd dig out his original statement. Almost invariably, I found that the original "prediction" bore scant resemblance to the later self-congratulation.

Sometimes the prediction was so hedged that almost any outcome would have made the forecaster a winner. In other cases, it wasn't a prediction or buying recommendation at all—merely a passing comment in the midst of a discussion of something else. Or the prediction was contradicted later by an entirely new forecast.

Of course, some forecasts *do* work out substantially as expected. Make enough of them and some are bound to come true. I've made a few myself, and I managed to dine out on them for years afterward.

But a winning forecast usually comes buried in a bundle of

predictions—most of which will go awry. How can you know in advance which of the many forecasts will pay off?

The simple truth is this: When your precious wealth is on the line, you can't rely on anyone to foresee the zigs and zags of the markets.

## Forecasters Should Be
## Fabulously Wealthy

Most forecasters freely admit that their records aren't perfect. Typically, one will say, "No one has a crystal ball, but I've been right more often than most people." This encourages an unrealistic assumption—that there are *degrees* of success in forecasting. In other words, forecasting may produce big benefits or lesser benefits.

But that isn't really true. If you think about it, you realize that forecasting actually is an all-or-nothing business: *Forecasts either are profitable or they aren't.* As with pregnancy, there are no shades of gray.

Can a forecaster make a significant profit predicting the future or can't he? If the answer is no, why should I pay attention to his predictions? If the answer is yes, we may have some business to discuss.

If he can forecast the future, he should be rich. No, not just rich—*very, very* rich. I don't mean he should have accumulated a paltry million dollars or so. I mean he should have accumulated a quarter billion, $2 billion, $5 billion, or more. In fact, he should own his own country.

Why not? If he can forecast the investment markets

reliably, his profits should be at least 50% a year—if not 100% or more—because there are plenty of ways to profit in up markets, down markets, and even sideways markets. If he could guarantee even 25% a year consistently, year after year, he'd be one of the most sought-after investment advisors in the world.

It wouldn't matter if he had no capital to start with. There are people and companies out there with piles of money—George Soros, Bank of America, Goldman Sachs, and hundreds more—who would eagerly put up $100 million or more to profit from his genius.

So why, then, isn't Rupert Murdoch or Fidelity Funds beating down his doors? He might say they don't know about his talents. But why not? They have every reason to seek out anyone so talented, wherever he may be.

Or he might say they refuse to believe he can do what he says. But if he can't prove to *them* he can forecast the future profitably, why should *we* believe him? There's nothing vague about investment trades: Every buy or sell order has an established price and identifiable transaction costs. So it's easy enough to determine whether the forecaster provides profitable recommendations. If he's truly successful, he can prove it to anyone.

Of course, if all he does is toss off a laundry list of predictions every January and then revisit the few winners a year later, we're not talking about the real world or real money. It's simply a parlor game—*Masters of the Universe* for would-be investors. In that case, he should play the game and have fun, but he shouldn't ask you to listen to him or to allow him to make your investment decisions.

If someone really could predict economic events, he could make a new fortune every year by warning companies about the plans and future actions of competitors. He could own a large part of the world within a decade or two.

So you aren't likely to find him wasting his time in a brokerage office, chatting in an Internet investing forum, writing books or newsletters, or advising politicians.

## The Benefits of Forecasting

Forecasts are not entirely useless. Someone's predictions can help you recognize that your own expectations for the future aren't the only possible outcome. This can help keep you humble and prudent.

And a forecast might call attention to a potential future that others are ignoring. If you come to feel a given event is quite possible but most people disagree with you, the market probably will provide a big payoff if you bet on that event and prove to be right. So if you like to watch the investment markets closely and you see a potential future that most people are ignoring, you may want to make a small speculation with money you can afford to lose.

But the key word is "potential." No one can foresee the future reliably. No future is inevitable. No event *has* to happen.

And a sure way to lose what you've accumulated is to risk the funds that are precious to you on the idea that some event *is* inevitable.

## Beware the Fortune-Teller

Investment profits come not from foreseeing events, but from an investment strategy that prepares you for everything—to capitalize on the good things that happen and to be protected against the bad, to be able to handle surprises without being hurt.

Rule #11 provides such a strategy.

I've spent a good deal of space on this subject, because forecasting is at the heart of investing for so many people. But what you would never pay attention to elsewhere is no more appropriate when handling your investments.

# More about
# Relying on an Investment Expert

The *Hulbert Financial Digest* monitors the portfolios of several hundred popular investment newsletters, taking note of every buy and sell recommendation—to determine precisely how profitable the newsletter writer's advice has been. Each issue names the newsletters with the best recent results.

But (surprise!) *the leaders keep changing.* Last year's genius rarely returns to the head of the pack this year.

During the 1980s I made it a point to pay close attention to the results *Hulbert* reported. There were some very revealing examples of what can happen when you expect last year's winners to repeat their victories for your benefit.

For example, one newsletter writer compiled the #1 profit record in 1985—and even repeated that feat in 1986. What better assurance could you want going into 1987? But in 1987 the writer lost 58% of his customers' capital in the month of October alone, when the stock market crashed.

Well, perhaps two years of success was too brief to assure the advisor's reliability. But the lists of long-term winners are just as volatile. The newsletter with the best record for the latest 5-year period might not be anywhere near the top of next year's 5-year list.

And if you look at lists showing the advisors with today's best 5-year, 6-year, and 7-year records, you might be surprised at how different the lists are. Just changing the starting date of a track record can make a considerable difference in the result.

Here's another example: In September 1987 the *Hulbert Financial Digest* published a study of newsletter performance for the 7-year period from the *Digest's* inception at June 30, 1980, through June 30, 1987. The newsletter with the #1 record for the seven years was a little-known publication that had compiled a gain of exactly 600%—which is a compound profit of 32% per year.

Now that's a remarkable record. And it wasn't for just one or two years. The record covered seven years—a period that included high inflation, falling inflation, high interest rates, falling interest rates, a very bad recession, and good times. Had you read that study in September 1987, you'd have had good reason to think you'd found an advisor who could beat the market in any economic environment.

But if you started acting on this newsletter's recommendations immediately, you would have lost 57% of your capital *the first month*—again because of the 1987 stock market crash.

Of course, even after that one terrible month, the advisor still had a 200% gain from 1980 through 1987. And it's the long-term result that matters, right?

But the long-term result was irrelevant to you—and to nearly all of his readers. Hardly anyone had followed the newsletter's advice since 1980, because hardly anyone knew it existed in 1980. Only *after* the winning record was compiled did the newsletter writer become known and investors begin acting on his advice.

Of course, the two examples I've given were each affected by the 1987 stock market crash. You might feel the crash was an extraordinary event that excuses any advisor's losses. But are you willing to rely on someone who doesn't allow for the possibility of an extraordinary incident? How do you know there won't be a crash or some other exceptional event next month?

In fact, the 1987 crash provides a good example of another way track records can mislead. In 1997 the *Hulbert Financial Digest* showed how a newsletter's performance record depended on whether you started the record just before the stock market crash or just after it.

For example, as of October 1997, one prominent newsletter's 10-year gain was 27.1% per year, far outstripping the average stock's gain of 17.5%. But just two months earlier, the same newsletter's 10-year record showed a yearly gain of only 12.7%—slightly less than the 13.3% annual return for the average stock. It all depended on whether the October 1987 stock market crash was part of the ten years.

As Mark Hulbert pointed out, "When you pick a newsletter on the basis of ten years that don't include a bear market, you're implicitly assuming that the next ten years won't include one either."[1]

Mutual-fund records can be just as misleading. Investors spend a lot of time and trouble poring over the track records of funds. But last year's record is no indication of next year's result.

Forgive me for reaching back so far in time, and for using such an extreme example, but I have to tell you about Strate-

---

[1] "1987's Lingering Impact," the *Hulbert Financial Digest*, August 25, 1997, page 1. The stock market gains are for the S&P 500 Index with dividends reinvested. It's interesting to note that the S&P 500 Index outperformed the average of the 13 prominent newsletters used in the *Hulbert* study—no matter which starting date was used. Information on the *Hulbert Financial Digest* can be found on page 166.

gic Capital Gains. It had the #1 performance record out of 973 funds monitored for the final calendar quarter of 1985. The very next quarter, the fund finished 973rd—dead last.[2]

Why do such reversals of fortune happen? Because spectacular winning streaks come as much from luck as from talent. Out of the tens of thousands of investment advisors and funds, mere chance dictates that a few of them will be riding lucky streaks on any day.

And those are the ones you'll hear about. When an investment advisor's luck is good, he becomes a celebrity, he attracts a crowd of new clients, and then his luck turns bad.

The one sure thing about luck is that it changes eventually.

Fortunately, while you may need an advisor to act as a Helper, you don't need an advisor to act as a Market-Beater.

---

[2] The performance records were compiled by Lipper Analytical Services, and published in Barron's, May 19, 1986, page 47.

# More about
# Trading Systems

We rely on a multitude of cause-and-effect relationships in everyday life. The light comes on when you flip a switch; the TV comes to life when you click on the remote control. Why can't we count on such firm relationships in the investment world?

Because lights and TV sets operate with physical elements—particles, forces, masses, substances, structures—that are uniform and constant. Every electron is identical to every other electron—yesterday, today, and tomorrow—and each one is a perfect specimen.

Investment prices flow from the actions of *people*—human beings who think and learn and pursue individual goals, including goals that often aren't clearly defined. Each person is different, and each person changes in some way every day.

Thus history might repeat itself exactly when you flip the light switch, but it's unlikely to do so for any economic or investment indicator that underlies a trading system.

## Track Records

Because the builder of a trading system expects human beings to be as consistent as light bulbs, he believes that whatever his computer discovers about past relationships will hold good for the future.

To demonstrate the value of his great discovery, he will compile a track record showing how much money you would have made if you had only used the system over the past umpteen years.

When you see that track record, you might assume that he has been using the system himself for those umpteen years, and that all those dollars you could have made are dollars he *did* make. But in fact he's saying only that if you (or he or Butch Cassidy or anyone else) had happened to use the system, that lucky person would have made so many millions.

But unfortunately for you, him, Butch Cassidy, and everyone else, no one knew about the system umpteen years ago. The relationship was discovered only in retrospect.

So when you run across a system that sports a wonderful track record, keep in mind the possibility that you will be the first person to use it. It will be one small step for mankind, but perhaps a giant step off a cliff for you.

## Never, Never (Happened) Land

I once saw a magazine ad offering professional money management.

The ad contained a graph covering 1977 through 1986. It showed that the S&P 500 Index rose 266% during those 10 years. But the gain in the S&P was dwarfed by an investment that seemed to be ascending to the heavens. The headline in the graph said "2,806% in Ten Years."

Wow! Can you imagine making 2,806% on your money in just ten years? (That would run $10,000 into $290,600.)

There is, however, a footnote. With a very good magnifying glass, I was able to make out the small print, which said:

> Based upon an initial investment of $100,000 on January 1, 1977, utilizing an equally weighted investment portfolio of 10 of the top-performing no-load mutual funds as determined on a year-to-year basis including reinvestment of dividends. The graph is intended solely to illustrate the exceptional performance which theoretically could be obtained by carefully selecting top performing mutual funds for an investment portfolio as opposed to the S&P 500. This graph is not intended to imply that the above performance has been or will be achieved in the [*name withheld to protect the guilty*] program and past performance is not necessarily indicative of future results.

In other words, the advisor didn't produce a gain of 2,806% over 10 years. He didn't even claim he *would have* produced such a result using his current system—or any other system.

The graph merely showed what would have happened if, each year, you somehow could have known in advance which 10 mutual funds would be the best performers for the coming year and bet your money on them.

Yes, and if my aunt had whiskers, she would be my uncle.

I eagerly await the appearance of an ad with the headline "Do You Sincerely Want to Have $3,012,110,000,000?"

A footnote will explain:

Based upon the value of all shares on the New York Stock Exchange, the American Stock Exchange, and the over-the-counter market. This hypothetical wealth figure is intended solely to illustrate how much money you would have if you could buy every share of stock in America. It is not intended to imply that you could acquire every share of stock in existence using the Foley Foolproof Fluctuation Formula, or that anyone has become rich using the Formula, or that anyone has ever used the Formula, or that we have figured out yet what the Formula is. But we'd like you to trust us with your money anyway.

The creativity and daring of the investment world is truly amazing. There is no end to the ideas that the world's hottest hands will place in your mailbox.

But all the "would haves" and "could haves" in the world won't make a dime for you.

## Systems and Indicators

Systems and indicators assume an essentially static world—in which all movement is merely a deviation from, or a return to, norms that remain the same year after year, even century after century. But in fact we live in a world in which the underlying causes of prices—technology, human wants, and existing resources—change constantly.

Thus no track record, covering the past, can tell you what works today; no indicator can foretell market movements; no system can take the uncertainty out of investing; and no investment can truly promise a profit without threatening a loss.

You may find a system of trading that doesn't seem to have the flaws I've discussed here. When you do, I won't be there to rain on your parade. So please try to remember that no system is riskless, and that no indicator can give you an inside track to the future.

The first principle of trading systems is:

*The system that has worked perfectly up to now will go sour when you stake your money on it.*

# More about Investing
# on a Cash Basis

Debt is dangerous because it magnifies and speeds up losses—which won't be limited to just the cash you've invested.

With a margin account for stocks, bonds, or commodities, you can wind up losing more than you invested. Even though a broker is supposed to notify you when your equity is getting too thin, the price can drop so suddenly that your equity falls below zero.

Borrowing to buy real estate can be less dangerous, but only if you're careful.

A non-recourse mortgage means that the lender's only method of enforcing the loan is to foreclose on the property. You're not obligated to repay the loan any other way. If you default on the mortgage and the property is sold for less than the amount of the mortgage, you aren't required to make up the difference. Thus with non-recourse financing you can never lose more than you actually lay out in cash.

In some states, non-recourse mortgages are mandated by law—and all lenders understand in advance that a borrower won't make up the difference if a foreclosed property can't be sold for enough to pay off the mortgage.

This factor is built into the interest rate and the other terms of the mortgage, so a borrower who walks away from a mortgage isn't taking advantage of the lender. The foreclosure still becomes a part of your record, but it won't bankrupt you.

If you want to use borrowed money—in any kind of transaction—do so only if your liability is limited strictly to the amount you put up in cash.

Even then, however, realize that the debt magnifies the amount you can lose on any drop in price. So limit your investment so that your maximum possible loss is too small to harm your standard of living or your future.

# More about Making
# Your Own Decisions

Getting someone to manage your money conservatively and safely seems simple enough.

But in practice it's easier to decide how to invest prudently yourself than to decide to whom you could safely delegate decision-making authority.

The traditional guidelines for finding the right advisor always seem simple enough:

- Deal only with a reputable firm.

- Find someone well-known and highly regarded in the investment profession and, if local, well-respected in your community.

- Get references.

- Deal with someone recommended by an individual you respect.

But, in fact, these guidelines don't really work out in practice.

Firms that are reputable and highly regarded seem to go broke at about the same rate as companies you've never heard of. Pan American Airways, Chrysler, Drexel Burnham Lambert, and other companies were highly regarded before they got into trouble. Even the U.S. government once had a pretty good reputation.

References tell you only that a few people have been satisfied with an advisor or a firm. And since those references are supplied by the person you're considering, they don't reveal how many disgruntled former customers there might be.

And the recommendations of people you respect don't mean much. What do they know about choosing an investment advisor? They can be wrong as easily as you can.

So it comes back to relying on yourself—not to pick a decision-maker, but to make your own investment decisions.

Use the advice and suggestions of writers and advisors as jumping-off points—ideas to consider and to stimulate your own thinking. But you must be the final judge of what you will do with your savings.

## Who's More Likely to Make a Rational Decision for You?

Many fairy tales are circulated about the cool, professional savvy of money managers—compared with the emotion-driven, easily panicked "small investors" who supposedly have the habit of moving in the wrong direction at any given time.

But in fact the professionals who manage the large pension funds and investment companies are no different. They, too, are frequently driven by emotion—as we all are at times. We're told often that the markets are ruled by "fear and greed"; if that's true, there's no reason to think the pros have been vaccinated against those emotions.

Most professionals are herd animals. They work together, have lunch together, ride the same trains to the city, read the same research, talk endlessly about investments together, and come to the same conclusions a large part of the time. Their thinking is inbred. Consequently, the pros often are pack animals—running together in one direction or another.

A professional money manager wants his performance record to be as good as possible, of course. But his chief concern is to outdo his competitors—or at least not to lag behind them. His principal fear isn't that he might show a loss with your money or that he might miss a golden opportunity, but that a competitor might outperform him and get your account.

If the market drops suddenly, he—just like anyone else—is afraid of getting out too soon and looking like a fool for panicking. He, too, has heard over and over about the people who sold out at the bottom of the 1987 crash—just before the market rallied. But once his competitors start running for the exits, he has nothing to lose by running with them—and everything to lose by staying behind. In other words, his decision can be driven by fear.

Any individual investor probably lets his ego and other extraneous elements dictate investment decisions sometimes. But, no matter how much or how little money he has, an individual investor worries most about achieving his investment goals. His chief concern is that his investments are building a secure retirement for himself—not that he's keeping up with his fellows, nor that he looks good to others. In many cases, he's more likely to make a sober judgment about getting into or out of a market than a professional will.

This is borne out whenever there's a sudden drop in the stock market. Small investors generally don't panic and rush to cash in their mutual fund shares. But the mutual funds themselves (run by professionals) usually start selling off their stock positions—only to buy them back later at higher prices.

For years and years, "savvy" investment writers have been telling us about the coming Armageddon—the day when all the novices will panic and run for the exits at once, crowding the doors so that you won't be able to get out. But time after time, the stage has been set for such a stampede—and only the professionals have panicked.

## Insiders

And, finally, if you're looking for someone who will always know what to do, "insiders" are no more help than fortune-tellers or high-priced pros.

In 1970, the chief gold trader at the largest Swiss bank told a friend of mine that the gold price would never go above $40. When asked how he could be so sure, the trader replied, "Because we control the market."[1]

---

[1] Shortly thereafter the gold price started rising, and within ten years it peaked at $850.

**RULE #9**

# More about
# Understanding What You Do

If you deal directly with a financial planner or investment advisor who proposes a particular investment or program, and if you don't understand it fully, ask him to explain it for you step by step.

If it's still unclear, ask to have the investment explained again. If you can't follow it on the second go-round, it definitely isn't for you.

However, it may be something you'll understand later. If it seems important to you, perhaps a broker or advisor can provide literature that explains the investment—or you can obtain a book that will teach you what you need to know.

But until you're sure you understand exactly how the investment works, stay clear of it.

Realize, too, that sometimes the problem only seems to be your ignorance or lack of sophistication, when in fact you're being offered an investment or a plan that truly doesn't make sense. Some people might be less discerning than you—or more inclined to assume something makes sense just because they've heard other people praise it.

It doesn't really matter whether they're wrong or you're dense. If you can't understand it, don't do it.

# More about Spreading the Risk

It's easy to believe that some institutions will always be there for us.

For example, the U.S. government guarantees each bank account up to $100,000 through the Federal Deposit Insurance Corporation (FDIC). But the FDIC doesn't have nearly enough in reserve to stop a large bank run or widespread bank failures.

The savings-and-loan scandals more than exhausted the resources of the Federal Savings and Loan Insurance Corporation (FSLIC), and Congress had to appropriate additional money out of the general fund.

We have no way of knowing what the response will be if Congress is asked to bail out the FDIC someday. Perhaps conditions will be put on your access to your bank accounts—as they were in the 1930s. We have no way of knowing, and slogans that say "Congress will never let the banks fail" are no substitute for real security.

We live in an uncertain world, and surprises are the norm. You shouldn't risk the chance that a single surprise will wipe out a large part of your holdings.

You can protect yourself against the possibility of institutional crisis by using more than one institution.

You can protect yourself against the failings of individuals by relying only on yourself.

And you can protect yourself against investment roller coasters by diversifying across investment markets. Each investment has its time to shine and its time to suffer—and no one can consistently foresee the turning points in advance.

Protection comes from diversification, assuring that no single event can destroy you—and from balance, assuring that what is bad for one investment you hold may be very good for other investments you hold.

**RULE #11**

# More about
# the Bulletproof Portfolio

The Permanent Portfolio plan I outlined in Part I is a realistic way for you to obtain safety and profit without becoming an investing expert.

The portfolio combines simple investments to achieve the balance needed to protect against whatever may come—while earning solid gains during most any kind of economic environment. Although your curiosity might encourage you to check the results of the portfolio periodically, you need attend to it only once a year.

The rest of the time, you can get on with your work, your family, and the things that interest you more. This truly is a portfolio you can walk away from—confident that it will take care of you through good times and bad.

## How to Invest

The method of investing in each of the four categories will be critical to the success of the portfolio.

In each of the four categories, you must invest in a way that enables that category to pull the entire portfolio upward when its time comes. It doesn't matter so much that this also will make the category a loser when the investment is out of favor. In most years, at least one investment will be a loser, but the other investments should more than make up for any losses.

Here we will set the guidelines for investing in each of the four categories. The appendix "Where to Get Help" beginning on page 155 lists a number of specific companies that match the qualifications given here.

## Stocks

To profit when stocks are in a broad upward market, your holdings must represent the entire market—not selected industries, which might happen to be left behind.

The easiest and most effective way to do this is to split the 25% stock-market portion among three mutual funds.[1]

Choose funds that invest in a broad cross-section of stocks—and that remain fully invested in stocks at all times, rather than trying to pick the best times to own stocks. You would defeat the purpose of the portfolio if you expected a fund manager to foresee the winners in next year's market or to move in and out of the market according to his views of the future. You aren't asking a mutual fund to speculate for you.

In addition, you want funds that invest in volatile stocks, in the hope that they will move farther than the general stock market when times are good.

Use three funds if possible, rather than one, so that you're protected against any mistakes an individual fund might make.

[1] A mutual fund is an investment company that invests your money for you by buying a large selection of stocks, bonds, or other liquid investments—normally limiting itself to one type of investment.

You buy shares in the mutual funds directly from the funds themselves. When I selected funds for the Permanent Portfolio, I applied five standards to each fund:

1. *Fully invested:* It should remain virtually fully invested at all times. This is vital, since the Permanent Portfolio is supposed to remain invested in all four investment categories at all times. If a fund has only 85% or so of its assets invested from time to time, that's not critical. But don't buy a fund that might drop to 70%, 50%, or less when its managers are bearish, because you'd be betting on the fund managers' timing skills.

2. *Broadly Invested:* It should be invested across the whole market, rather than in selected sectors, so that the fund will move up and down as the stock market itself moves up and down.

3. *No commissions:* It should be a no-load fund. Since there are more than enough such funds, there's no need to pay commissions when you buy or sell.[2]

4. *Minimum investment:* Most funds require a minimum amount to open an account. You need a fund whose minimum investment is no greater than 8% of your total portfolio—as you will want to give it one third of the 25% stock-market portion.

5. *Reliability:* The first two points should be a matter of fixed policy for the fund, so that it won't change its strategy next year. Also, the fund should be old enough to

---

[2] A "load" is a commission you pay when you buy or sell the fund. A no-load fund has no commissions (or it has commissions of insignificant size).

show that it does carry out these policies consistently, and also that it isn't—for some other reason—a consistent loser.

The appendix on page 156 lists eight funds I believe are suitable for a Permanent Portfolio. They were chosen by the standards above, not because I believe they will be the top-performing funds next year (since no one can know that). Call them to receive free information and an application form.

One virtue of a Permanent Portfolio is that it doesn't require constant monitoring and tinkering. So I haven't changed my fund recommendations since the mid-1980s.

## Bonds

For the bond portion, you don't want to have to monitor credit risk, so buy only U.S. Treasury bonds. So long as the U.S. government has the ability to tax people or print money to pay its bills, there is virtually no credit risk (although the bonds can fall in price or lose purchasing power to inflation).

The Treasury has issued a series of bonds that mature (will be paid off) at various dates over the next 30 years. The longer the time to maturity, the greater effect changes in interest rates have on the bond's price.

Since there may be times when the bond category will have to carry the entire Permanent Portfolio, you want a bond with the potential for big price movements. So put the 25% in the Treasury bond issue that currently has the longest time until it matures. That will be close to 30 years. Ten years later, the bond will have only 20 years to maturity; at that time re-place it with a new 30-year bond.

The minimum Treasury bond purchase is $1000. You can buy the bonds through a commercial bank or a stockbroker.[3]

## Gold

Gold is the best inflation hedge because it's much more pow-erful and reliable than any other investment that might react favorably to inflation. Whatever the inflation rate (once it reaches 6% or so), gold will respond much more powerfully than any other investment.

To get the full advantage of gold, hold gold itself—not gold stocks or collectors' coins, either of which could move in the opposite direction from gold under some conditions.

Buy *bullion* coins—coins whose only value is the gold bul-lion they contain. They sell for about 3–5% more per ounce than gold bullion. That means a one-ounce coin will sell for about $310–$315 if the price of gold is $300 an ounce.[4]

You can buy the coins from a local coin dealer (listed in the Yellow Pages), from many stockbrokers, and from national coin companies. A few national companies are listed in the ap-pendix on page 161. Call three dealers to get quotes and then buy from the one with the best price or most convenience.

---

[3] If you object to investing in government securities, use long-term corporate bonds with AAA credit ratings that have no call provisions. (A call provision allows the bond-issuer to pay off the bond early, which reduces the potential for price rises that you want in a long-term bond.)

[4] The 3–5% bonus is a premium you pay for having the gold in a recognizable pack-age that needs no assaying. You generally get the premium back when you sell a coin.

## Cash

The cash portion should be kept in a money market fund investing only in short-term U.S. Treasury securities, so that you don't have to evaluate credit risk. These securities are safer than bank accounts and other debt instruments.[5]

If your cash budget is large enough, divide your holdings between two or three funds—for further protection against the unthinkable.

On page 159 you'll find four funds that are fully invested in Treasury bills, and that don't dilute the safety of their holdings in any way.

## Tax Considerations

You don't have to get fancy to minimize taxes on your investments. The Permanent Portfolio itself is a fairly low-tax investment plan.

The stock market mutual funds are devoted more to rising share prices than dividend payments, so there may not be a lot of currently taxable income in the stock market portion. Gold produces no dividends or interest (its gains come in price increases), which means it produces no current tax liability.

Treasury bills (or a money market fund) produce interest income each year, which is fully taxable. So if you have an IRA, Keogh, 401(k), or other pension plan, that would be the best

[5] A money market fund is a mutual fund that invests your money in short-term vehicles (such as bank CDs or other debt instruments) that pay interest.

place to keep the cash portion. This allows the interest to compound tax-free for many years.

Bonds also pay interest twice yearly, in addition to offering potential price gains. So if the cash portion doesn't fill your pension plan entirely, use the remaining space for the bonds.[6]

## Getting Started with Very Little

You can start a Permanent Portfolio with very little capital.

If you have at least $1,000, but less than $4,000, you can begin by investing in a mutual fund, the Permanent Portfolio Fund, that itself holds diversified investments of the kind I've described. It is explained on page 162.

With as little as $4,000, you can buy the individual investments directly, which is always preferable. The $4,000 threshold exists because each of the four components must get a full 25% of the total—and one Treasury bond will cost about $1,000. In addition, many mutual funds and money market funds require a minimum investment of $1,000.

With capital beyond $4,000, you can achieve greater diversification within each category. At $12,000, for example, you can have $1,000 in each of three mutual funds (for the 25% stock budget) and each of three money market funds (for the 25% cash budget).

With greater amounts of capital, you can diversify geographically—perhaps having some of your holdings out-

---

[6] A further discussion of ways to use tax-reduction vehicles for your Permanent Portfolio begins on page 129.

side your own country, to insulate yourself from whatever might happen at home.

Whatever you do, however, don't defeat the purpose by making the program so complicated that it becomes burden-some to maintain. The Permanent Portfolio should relieve your anxieties, not add to them. If you find that it is becoming too much work to keep track of it, you've let it become too complicated.

It's as important to keep it simple as it is to keep it safe.

## Real Estate

Some people think of real estate as an investment. And, of course, it *is* possible to buy a home and later resell it at a higher price.

But no matter how much your home has appreciated when you sell it, it's quite possible that you'll replace it with another home in the same higher price range. And real estate isn't in the same world as stocks, bonds, gold, or cash. The differences between them and real estate are numerous and important.

First, even if you buy a home primarily as an investment, you probably will select a particular house based on its value as your residence—rather than by any standards of investment analysis.

Second, you can choose the dollar amount your Perma-nent Portfolio should have in stocks, bonds, gold, and cash. But real estate doesn't work that way. You can't shop for a res-idence that happens to fit exactly the dollar amount you've al-located for real estate in an investment portfolio.

Further, when price changes push the portfolio out of balance (too much of one investment and too little of another), you can buy or sell a specific amount of stocks, bonds, or gold. But you can't sell your front porch or build a back porch just to adjust your home's value to the amount allocated for it in the portfolio.

The value of real estate in your portfolio is indivisible, and everything else must accommodate it. Just like a 15-foot piano in the living room, you have to arrange the rest of the furniture around it.

Third, most investments trade in markets from which you can obtain price quotes whenever you want them, so you know exactly what your holdings are worth. And when you want to sell, you can do so immediately. But you can't know the value of a piece of real estate until you actually sell it, and a sale can take a long, indefinite time.

For all these reasons, real estate—even your residence—sits in a Permanent Portfolio like a gorilla at a banquet. Its manners may be good, but somehow it just doesn't fit in.

So if real estate isn't an investment, what is it? One of three things.

It can be a consumption item—the place where you live and enjoy your life. Or it can be a business you go into—buying and selling properties, the way a furniture dealer buys and sells tables and chairs. Or it can be a speculation—something you play around with, using money you can afford to lose.

It can be any of those things. But it isn't an investment as we normally think of investments.

## Alternatives to the
## Permanent Portfolio

The Permanent Portfolio, despite the enormous safety it provides, is an investment plan that's simple enough for almost anyone to carry out.

But it's conceivable that you might find even this simple plan baffling. If so, what can you do?

First of all, realize that if a Permanent Portfolio is too complicated for you, you definitely have no business risking your money on anything that requires more extensive knowledge about investing. So you must be doubly resistant to the siren songs of hot schemes.

Here are some alternative approaches. None is as safe as the Permanent Portfolio I've recommended. But you can use one of them if you find the Permanent Portfolio too difficult for you—or if you need to do something temporarily until you have the time and opportunity to set up a true Permanent Portfolio. In order of safety, they are:

1. Buy shares in the Permanent Portfolio Fund, a mutual fund that diversifies among the Permanent Portfolio investments (plus a few others). The fund is explained on page 162.

2. Put all your savings in U.S. Treasury bills. A bank or stock broker can arrange this for you.

3. Divide your savings among savings accounts at three or more commercial banks.

## Using All Four Investments

For almost everyone, the Permanent Portfolio concept will be easy enough to handle.

As you set up your portfolio, remember you have no way to predict the future. No matter how well or poorly an investment has done recently, there's no way to know how well it will do next year or over the next five years.

So don't play games with your Permanent Portfolio. Don't wait for any investment to become cheaper before you buy it. And don't go overboard investing in something that happens to be doing well now.

Just put 25% in each of the four categories.

During the 1970s bonds plummeted in price as interest rates rose. In the early 1980s, some of my newsletter customers wouldn't buy bonds for the Permanent Portfolio—figuring they were a perpetual losing investment. They couldn't know that bonds had actually started a long-term uptrend in 1981.

By the mid-1980s some of them acknowledged that they should have bought bonds when they set up their portfolios. But, they reasoned, now bonds were higher in price—and they probably had gone about as high as they were going to. So they wanted to wait to buy at what they expected would be a lower price. But bonds continued to rise—more than doubling in price by the end of the 1980s.

The lesson was clear: No matter how strong your expectations about the near future, you could easily be mistaken. And the point of the Permanent Portfolio is to ignore your own expectations and let the portfolio take care of you no matter what may come.

In the 1990s I encountered the same resistance to buying gold for the portfolio. After all, it had gone nowhere in years—and it produced no interest or dividends.

But gold will revive—probably when we least expect it, and probably when we most need it. And when it does revive, you'll have no way of knowing whether its resurrection is just a temporary blip or the start of a new bull market. So you'll never be sure of the best time to add it to the portfolio—unless you add it now.

If you want to have a Permanent Portfolio, fund it with equal portions of all four investments and don't worry over which is going to do best. It is a *package* of investments that provides the safety you need. Tear apart the package and you tear apart the safety.

# More about Speculating

I've said you shouldn't speculate with money you can't afford to lose. But how do you decide how much that is? How much should you allocate to the Variable Portfolio?

The answer may be obvious to you. But if it isn't, pick an initial figure that seems reasonable, and then spend a few minutes imagining that you've lost it all.

What would the loss do to your life? Does the thought of losing the entire Variable Portfolio unnerve you? Would it change your future? Would it force you to change your lifestyle or your plans for retirement? If so, you've allocated too much to the Variable Portfolio. Repeat the exercise with a smaller amount.

On the other hand, if the loss doesn't seem like much, and if it doesn't seem like the amount allocated is enough to satisfy your urge for speculation, repeat the exercise with a larger amount. Once again, imagine that you've lost it all. Have you gone too far? Or can you increase the amount again?

When you've finally arrived at a figure that seems large enough to satisfy your appetite for speculation, but isn't large enough to endanger your future, you've identified the amount you should allocate to the Variable Portfolio.

Here's another approach: If you're already diverting a fixed percentage of your income to your savings, increase that amount for a period of time. Divert the extra savings to the

Variable Portfolio. That way you won't interfere with your normal savings and investments.

## Don't Transfer Money from the Permanent Portfolio

If you should happen to lose all the money allocated to the Variable Portfolio, find some less expensive entertainment. But don't replenish the Variable Portfolio by reaching into the Permanent Portfolio. That would put you on the road to ruin.

Instead, wait until you can accumulate a new fund of money from your regular income (without interfering with what you're setting aside for your future). Use that to start a new Variable Portfolio if you still have the itch.

*Don't touch the Permanent Portfolio.* It is your future. In other words, don't play with your seat belt.

## Speculative Strategy

Expert speculators are unusual people, and I'm not one of them. However, I will offer a few thoughts about speculating for your consideration.

Few successful speculators try to foresee the future. Their success comes more from a sound strategy than from a line on tomorrow. And a successful strategy allows you to be wrong frequently.

A good poker player doesn't expect to win every hand, and he doesn't presume to know what cards the other players hold. Instead he tries to win a big pot when he has a good hand, and to fold early when he has a bad hand.

In the same way, a good speculator doesn't expect to win every bet, and he doesn't presume to know what lies over the horizon. Instead he hopes to make as much as possible when things go his way, and to get out of a speculation quickly when it goes bad.

No matter how good his strategy, the top-notch poker player expects to hit a cold spell from time to time—when his straights will be topped by flushes, or when one hand after another is too weak to bet on. And a good speculator knows that even the best circumstances can produce losses, and that there will be stretches with no good circumstances.

Even a player with a natural talent for poker or speculating needs considerable practice to develop his skill and to understand fully the milieu in which he's operating. No simple system will substitute for the years of experience that feed the intuition of an able speculator.

You might have a feel for speculating. But it will take many years of success before you can be confident you're not just on a lucky streak. That's one reason you should speculate only with money you can afford to lose.

## The Information You Rely On

It is very unlikely that you'll ever have information about any investment's prospects that isn't available to every other investor and speculator.

Even if someone presumes to give you inside information, you can be quite sure that:

1. The information you receive won't be entirely accurate, because it probably has passed through several hands on its way to you.

2. The information already has been known to other people—people with the wealth to make large purchases that have pushed up the investment's price. The investment no longer will be a bargain, despite what you believe you know about it.

Don't expect to outperform the market with information not available to everyone. Your only hope is to interpret widely shared information more wisely—letting you anticipate events that will be a surprise to most others.

## How You Make Money Speculating

You can make money speculating only when your expectations differ considerably from the prevailing wisdom.

The stock market is the equivalent of a computer that registers everyone's opinion of each company's future and calculates a stock price accordingly. Thus today's price for a stock represents the consensus opinion of most investors regarding that company's prospects.

If your opinion matches the consensus, you won't make much money betting on the stock—because the price already reflects that opinion. If events turn out to be pretty much as you expect, the price will rise only a little. But if events don't live up to the consensus opinion, the price could drop drastically. In other words, you're betting a lot with the chance of making only a small profit.

The situation is almost the opposite if your opinion is considerably different from the consensus. In that case, the price is much lower than it would be if investors expected the same events you do. If those events transpire, the price should go up considerably. If you arrange in advance a way of getting out quickly if events begin to go against you, you're risking only a little while gaining the chance to make a large profit.

You can make good profits speculating only when you expect something quite different from what most everyone expects.

Before you speculate, ask yourself why you think your expectations are wiser than those of others. Do you have a good reason to think so?

## Professionals Don't Even Beat the Market

Before you get carried away, let me give you one last warning.

Even investment professionals don't generally beat the markets. The *Hulbert Financial Digest* tracks the results achieved by the published model portfolios of hundreds of investment newsletters—written by people who spend 8–12 hours a day watching and studying the investment markets.

Each year only a handful of newsletters outperforms the Dow Jones Industrial Average. And the handful changes from year to year, so there's no way to know which advisor will have a "hot hand" in the coming year.[1]

[1] Information on the *Hulbert Financial Digest* is given on page 166. Some of the results it has reported are on pages 89–91.

Professionals are consumed with the job of tracking investments, and they have easy access to far more information than you do. If they can't consistently beat the investment markets, how can you? The answer is: *You probably can't.*

That isn't to say no one ever made a fortune speculating. Some of us made small or large fortunes during the 1970s. And there are people who have managed to stay on the right side of the markets through most of a long speculating career.

But the latter are a rare breed. They are people who have a unique intuitive feel for the markets.

And some of them are just lucky. It's not unreasonable to expect one out of every 10,000 speculators to compile an amazing record.

Are you likely to be the one?

Are you likely to win the lottery?

# More about

# Keeping Some Assets Overseas

If you're a world-class drug dealer or tied up in a billion-dollar controversy with your own government, a foreign bank might be brought under considerable pressure to reveal information about your account. But if you're a typical middle-class individual, your foreign holdings will be as anonymous as a fish in the Atlantic Ocean.

A foreign account in any country outside your own is a tremendous improvement over having everything in your home country. But some countries are more hospitable than others. And some have legal traditions that protect your privacy.

I've always been partial to Switzerland and Austria, because each has a centuries-old tradition of respecting privacy and fending off inquiries from other governments.

Banks in these countries are more private than American banks—beginning with the inability of *anyone* to obtain information about the account from the bank. Inquiring minds can learn the details of your account only if you allow them to.

## Flexibility

Having some money outside the reach of the government gives you flexibility—and this is true even if the government knows you have a foreign account.

If your government ever becomes so oppressive as to outlaw foreign bank accounts, prohibit ownership of certain investments, or hinder anything else important to your finances, having assets outside your country gives you the freedom to decide what to do at the time. Talk to an attorney to see in what way, and for how long, you can drag your feet before bringing the money home. You may be able to wait it out for years.

Before the time runs out, you might decide to pack up and move elsewhere—in which case you'll be grateful you had assets that your government couldn't touch.

In any event, you will have preserved some independence to make your own decisions—rather than having them made for you by the government.

## The Best Way to Use a Foreign Bank

If you hold American investments such as stocks, mutual funds, bonds, money market funds, and Treasury bills at a foreign bank, the bank buys them for you from a U.S. firm. The assets are held in the United States in the name of the foreign bank or a foreign broker with whom the bank does business.

Thus there is no record in the United States of your ownership. But the assets are in America nonetheless, and subject to American law.

If you buy and hold gold through the foreign bank, the gold most likely will be stored within the bank itself. It will be completely independent of the U.S. financial system. So it makes the most sense to use the foreign bank for part of your gold holdings.

Whatever you decide to keep at the bank, be sure to have some of the same investment in your own possession—which you can use when you need to rebalance your portfolio back to its original percentages.

## Secrecy

If you want your foreign account to be completely secret, keep these guidelines in mind.

- Open the account in person—or send the letter to open the account, as well as the money, from outside your country. Don't use a personal check to open the account.

- Tell the bank it should send you no correspondence about the account. Thus you'll need to keep the transactions simple and infrequent, so you won't have to stay in touch with the bank.

- Keep in a secret account only an investment, such as gold, that produces no interest or dividends—so that you aren't earning current income that should be reported to the tax collector. Since your objective is privacy, you shouldn't complicate the matter by risking the consequences of tax evasion—which can be horrendous.

- Tell the bank to keep the gold in segregated custody, rather than mixed in with the gold of other customers. That way you're using the foreign bank simply as storage, not as a bank account. And so you shouldn't feel obligated to report it to your government. Pay several years of storage fees in advance.

## Other Forms of Privacy

There are other lawful ways to keep wealth private.

For example, you can buy gold coins at home and store them yourself. So long as you don't sell them, you haven't done anything you must report to the tax collector. You might also want to have some cash tucked away somewhere—for protection against the unforeseeable.

If you would like more privacy over your financial affairs, just making the decision to look for it probably will open your mind to alternatives you hadn't noticed.

# More about
# Tax-Reduction Plans

Many companies have pension plans in which each employee can select investments for his own account. In such a plan, you usually can choose among two or more investments to hold—and usually with the option to switch from one to another from time to time.

For example, the plan might allow you to choose among: (1) a mutual fund invested in stocks; (2) a mutual fund invested in bonds; and (3) a money market fund invested in one or more types of short-term debt instruments, similar to the cash budget of your Permanent Portfolio.

Although these investments might seem to be satisfactory components of the Permanent Portfolio, they generally are less than ideal. The stock mutual funds in many, but not all, cases don't mirror the broad stock market. The bond mutual funds generally are invested in corporate bonds that aren't as safe as Treasury bonds. And the money market funds usually aren't invested in Treasury bills, which have less credit risk than other types of debt instruments.

However, the tax-deferral benefit of using such a pension plan is too good to pass up—provided you don't have to invest in something that is clearly inappropriate for the Permanent Portfolio. If it's possible to use more than one of the investments offered, I would do so—to keep any one of them from dominating its own category within your Permanent Portfolio.

Outside the company pension plan, be sure to keep other holdings of each of the four components—and make sure those holdings are in the form I suggested on pages 108–118.

## How to Use the Pension Plans

Deciding which investments to hold in a pension plan and which to own directly depends largely on how each type of investment provides its return:

1. Some investments produce interest or dividends—income that is taxable immediately if you hold the investments outside a pension plan.

2. Some investments provide their profits solely through price appreciation, producing no interest or dividends—and so they incur tax only when you sell them.

3. Some investments are combinations of the first two types.

A pension plan can reinvest 100% of its earnings without losing anything to taxes. It's important not to waste this benefit by using the plan for Permanent Portfolio investments— such as gold—that generate little or no current income, while paying tax each year on income-producing investments sitting outside the plan.

To make the best use of a pension plan, fill it with investments for the Permanent Portfolio in the following order:

1. Treasury bills
2. Treasury bonds
3. Stock-market mutual funds
4. Gold

Treasury bills produce interest every year, and that interest is the only thing they generate. So they should be inside a pension plan, if possible.

Treasury bonds produce earnings in two ways:

1. Interest paid twice a year, which is taxable immediately if you hold the bonds directly, and

2. Gains from increases in the price of the bonds, which are taxable only when you sell some of the bonds (which you would do either to rebalance the portfolio, or every ten years to replace them with bonds that have a longer remaining life).[1]

Mutual funds produce much of their earnings from price increases—which are taxable only when you sell some of the shares of the funds in order to rebalance the portfolio or when the fund distributes some of its capital gains to you. The funds also produce some dividends which are taxable each year.

---

[1] Replacing bonds is explained on page 110.

Gold generates no taxable income—except when you sell some to rebalance the portfolio.

## Tax Shelters

There are more complicated methods of shielding income from taxes than those I've discussed. But many, if not most, of these schemes are incomprehensible if you don't have degrees in both law and accounting. These complicated tax schemes could easily include vulnerabilities and liabilities of which you're not aware.

To act on any of the plans would violate Rule #9, doing only what you fully understand. It is dangerous to get involved with these plans—and you shouldn't even consider them if you qualify for one of the simpler plans I've discussed.

A great deal of money has been lost by people who hoped to beat the tax system. The losses came from investments that provided special tax advantages but didn't make economic sense, or from tax shelters that were disallowed by the IRS—and that led to ruinous penalties and interest.

The simpler, effective, non-controversial plans allow you to make the most of your Permanent Portfolio, and they threaten no surprises that could scuttle your retirement plans.

## Jail Bait

You may encounter schemes that purport to eliminate all income taxes legally. These plans are based on misguided interpretations of the income tax rules, and they're dangerous.

The theories advanced by their proponents include one or more of following contentions:

- Congress has never passed a law requiring you to pay taxes

- The 16th Amendment (authorizing an income tax) was never actually ratified

- The Internal Revenue Code applies only to corporations, or that it doesn't apply to wages or salaries, or that it applies only in U.S. possessions like Guam or the Virgin Islands

- The IRS itself says that paying income tax is voluntary

- A legal obligation to file a return that could incriminate you violates the 5th Amendment to the Constitution

And there are other contentions.

It is beyond the scope of this book to examine these claims. Here let me make just two points.[2]

First, it doesn't matter whether you believe the income tax is "legal." Whether or not it is, many people who don't pay income tax are put in prison.

One of the best known promoters of these schemes has been in prison three times—each time for tax evasion. During his time in prison, he usually figures out what was wrong with his plan—and he comes out with a new, safer way of getting

---

[2] The report "The Untax Promise" by Daniel J. Pilla refutes many of the tax-evasion claims. Details of the book are on page 167 of this book.

around the system. He tries it—and eventually goes back to prison.

Many others who have tried these schemes have paid for it with prison time. If they want to do that to protest the income tax system, that's their privilege. Most of them, however, went to prison because they thought there was a way to evade taxes without danger.

No matter how strong the argument someone makes to claim you don't have to pay income tax, remember that the question isn't: Is the logic correct? The question is: Do people go to prison for following it? And they do. Is that what you want to risk?

Second, the claims usually are accompanied by stories of people who have followed the recommended procedure for years and have never been bothered by the IRS.

If the Internal Revenue Service is aware that you haven't paid your taxes for a year or two, it may send you a notice asking whether you've filed a return that they missed. If you don't answer and the IRS stops sending you notices, it isn't because the IRS has given up on you.

Instead, the IRS will identify you as a tax-evader. The next step is to give you enough rope to hang yourself. The IRS wants you to go several years without paying tax for two reasons: (1) to establish that it was part of a pattern of deliberate evasion, rather than an isolated mistake; and (2) to allow the unpaid taxes, penalties, and interest to accumulate to a size that makes it worth prosecuting you.

Although I haven't dealt with the details of the tax-evasion schemes here, please understand that I've been aware of them for many years, I've investigated them, and I've found no value whatsoever in any of them.

# More about

# Asking the Right Questions

Here are five more questions you shouldn't ask when considering an investment.

## Track Record

### 1. "How well did this investment perform in recent years?"

The only piece of wisdom I've ever heard from the U.S. government is the Securities and Exchange Commission's disclaimer that past performance is no guide to future success.

Investments have their ups and downs. And if you buy an investment after a few up years, you may be jumping in just in time for a few down years.

This is true as well of mutual funds, market timers, and other advisors.

What you need to know is:

- What kind of economic climate *should* cause this investment to prosper?

- In the past, *did* the investment prosper during that kind of climate?

- If the investment is for a balanced portfolio, will buying it give you too many investments dependent on that one kind of climate—making you too vulnerable to some other economic climate?

- If this investment is for a speculation, do you think we're heading into the economic climate that favors it?

## Taking the Plunge

### 2. "How much should I invest?"

No one can tell you how much to invest in anything because no one is in your circumstances, and no one can know exactly what you can handle.

If an investment is to contribute to a balanced portfolio, ask yourself:

- How much of the investment do I need to provide the proper balance against other investments in the portfolio?

- How big an investment would make me too vulnerable to some potential event?

If the asset is being considered as a speculation, ask yourself:

- Since the entire amount invested could be lost, how much can I afford to put into it?

## "Socially Responsible" Investing

### 3. "Is the company or mutual fund socially responsible?"

The stock exchange isn't a pulpit. If you want to promote a particular environmental policy, political philosophy, or other personal enthusiasm, do it with the profits you make from hardheaded investing.

Maximizing profits and furthering social policies are separate goals. Your investment decisions can serve only one master at a time. So it makes sense to focus on sound investing, and then—if you want—use the profits to support whatever cause excites you.

However, the management policy of a company or a fund is important in some cases. For example, if you buy a mutual fund to contribute to a Permanent Portfolio's balance, you're counting on the fund to perform in a certain way in various economic climates. You want to know that the investment will be just as appropriate next year as it is today. So ask:

- Is the management's policy a consistent one that you can count on—engraved in the fund's prospectus?

## Sponsors

### 4. "Who thinks this investment is about to rise?"

No one—not even the most astute investment advisor—knows how an investment will do next year. Anyone has about an even chance of being right when making a forecast for a particular investment.

It doesn't matter how good his record has been for picking stocks, timing the market, or spotting next year's winners. Never forget the first principle of investment advice:

*The investment advisor with the perfect record up to now will lose his touch as soon as you start acting on his advice.*

It does little good to know *who* is recommending an investment. The important questions are:

- *Why* is he recommending the investment? Do his arguments make sense?

- What will have to happen for his forecast to come true?

- What does he believe this investment adds to your portfolio?

- Is this something you might want to bet on with funds you can afford to lose?

## Popularity

### 5. "If this investment is so good, why don't I see it recommended in financial publications?"

As mentioned on page 122, unpopularity is essential to a speculation. So to make big profits, you have to feel a little lonely.

If the investment is being considered for the Permanent Portfolio, you have to decide whether it adds to *your* portfolio's safety. The recommendations you see in newsletters and magazines are made without any consideration for your particular needs or for the investment strategy presented in this book.

If someone discusses the investment you're considering, ask yourself:

- Is the advisor helping you decide whether the investment is right for you, or is he simply guessing whether the investment will go up in price?

If the latter, ignore the advice. If the former, and his information seems sound, take it into account when making your decision.

# More about
# the Pleasure Budget

You work all your life in order to reach a certain goal. When you arrive there, relax and enjoy it.

Make sure a sufficient part of your wealth is safe from all threats, and then don't worry over losing or wasting some part of the rest.

And don't worry about goals that other people may set for themselves. You don't have to accumulate more than you need to be secure. You don't have to be the biggest winner in the investment markets. You don't have to be anything but what you want for yourself and your family.

# More about
# Erring on the Side of Safety

Some people may tell you that you can't afford to play it safe—or even that economic conditions have made once-safe alternatives too risky.

They may say that unfamiliar investments and new strategies are your only hope for survival. For example, we heard often in the 1970s that the "poor sheep" who left their life savings in banks would lose everything to inflation. As it turned out, those poor sheep managed to survive.

Over the decade of the 1970s, inflation averaged 7.4% per year. The poor soul with money in a bank passbook savings account earned an average of only 4.8% per year—not enough to keep up with inflation.

So, for the worst financial decade since the 1930s, it cost the individual 2.6% of the purchasing power of his capital each year (23% for the decade) to avoid alien investment strategies and continue to do what was familiar.

That wasn't a good bargain. But, for someone with limited knowledge and a strong desire to keep most of what he had, it wasn't ruinous—not as bad as the losses that could have come from playing with investments he didn't understand.

And safety could have been considerably cheaper with almost any other simple strategy—such as leaving one's money in Treasury bills (which would have cost only 0.2% per year in purchasing power), or keeping just a tiny, fixed share of one's capital in gold coins.

With any of these simple approaches, the unsophisticated investor could hold on to all or most of his capital—and perhaps even make a little.

Meanwhile, many people who thought they were being sophisticated lost heavily by buying precious metals or real estate at the wrong time with borrowed money (expecting to repay it later with "cheaper dollars")—or trying to master the art of short-selling in the stock market or day-trading in the commodity market—or buying exotic investments such as strategic metals, diamonds, or colored gemstones—or trusting international money managers who turned out to be better promoters than managers.

As you know, I'm not suggesting you leave all your money in the bank, or even in T-bills—or in any one investment. That approach has its own risks and drawbacks. Nor am I saying that it was wrong to buy precious metals or real estate.

I *am* saying that history provides no evidence that only the bold and adventurous survive financially. I am suggesting that you stay clear of stampedes into investments you don't understand. I am saying you should ignore anyone who says your only route to financial survival is with an investment or strategy that scares you.

It's true that some people made fortunes in precious metals in the 1970s. And many people coped with inflation in ways that allowed them to hang on to all of what they had. But it's unlikely that anyone in either group played with investment strategies he didn't understand or couldn't easily execute.

You aren't a failure if you miss the boat. If you're not sure about the situation, just let the opportunity pass you by. The world won't end tomorrow. There will be more opportunities.

> *When in doubt about an investment decision, it is always better to err on the side of safety.*

# Epilogue:

# Getting On
# with Your Life

Now you have the 17 rules.

I hope they have armed you against all those serpents in the garden that will beckon you to stray from the straight and narrow investment path—attractions such as compelling forecasts, sure things, can't-lose systems, arrogance, scary stories, rosy scenarios, inside information, and hot tips from the homeless.

The rules are simply common sense. But most investors violate them frequently—even investors who are concerned primarily with safety.

They hope to find safety by following the advisor with a perfect forecasting record. Or they're persuaded to invest too much in one thing by a plausible "proof" that only one future is possible—because of the size of the federal debt, or because it's an election year, or because powerful people wouldn't let it be otherwise.

Many investors pay dearly for thinking the future is knowable. And when they lose a chunk of their life savings, there's always an excuse—an unprecedented turn in the market, a surprising change in government policy, or simply bad luck.

But they don't notice that they didn't have to be vulnerable to those things. They needed only to recognize that they live in an uncertain world, and that the commonsense rules in this book would have protected them.

## You Know as Much as They Do

When things go wrong, investors sometimes search for a new secret that will arm them against their latest mistakes. But they rarely discover the really important secret—the best-kept secret in the investment world:

*Almost nothing turns out as expected.*

Forecasts rarely come true, trading systems don't produce the results advertised for them, investment advisors with phenomenal records of success fail to deliver when your money is on the line, the best investment analysis is contradicted by actual events.

The secret—that things rarely work out as expected—is shared unwittingly by investors, brokers, advisors, newsletter writers, and financial journalists, few of whom can bring themselves to acknowledge it.

Each wants to appear to be in command of the situation, on top of the markets, aware of what's happening and what's going to happen—and to appear as though everything that has already happened was anticipated.

A professional needs to keep up this guise because he must look sharper than his competitors. Even investors often pose as members of the all-knowing—perhaps because no one wants to appear to be the only loser, and everyone else seems to be so smart.

And so everyone plays his part in protecting the secret. Forecasts are made and forgotten. Track records are displayed and never examined. Infallible systems lose money but are never questioned out loud. Many investment advisors continue to practice what really are superstitions, but no one calls them that. Financial experts keep explaining the present and the future, even though very little of what they said last year would sound reasonable now—if we could even remember what they said.

Most investors go on expecting the future to evolve in a predictable fashion, positive that some other people have found a reliable system of anticipating it. They keep searching for the Holy Grail, but they never find it.

At some point, investors have to ask themselves: *What's the point?* What practical good is accomplished by all the analysis, the anticipations, the forecasts?

## A Better Way

I've studied economics for the past forty years. So I'm well aware of how increased debt leads to higher interest rates and possibly inflation, how tax hikes retard the economy, how technology fuels economic growth, and other cause-and-effect relationships. Still, the events I anticipate don't seem to arrive on schedule—or even arrive at all, for that matter.

Of course, there are advisors who have great stories to tell about the important events they foresaw. But they never tell you about the many expected events that never happened.

The beginning of investment wisdom is to accept that we live in an uncertain world, and that we can never have enough information to know for certain why the market went up or down today—let alone what it's going to do tomorrow. We know only a little about the present—and much less about the future.

No one can tell you when the stock market will peak, how far it will fall, or which market group will lead the way back up. Human beings aren't able to foresee the future in any useful way. For every example cited of an investment forecast that came true, I can point to five that didn't—some of which may have come from the same forecaster.

Only when you abandon the hope that some advisor, some system, some source of inside tips is going to give you a short-cut to wealth, do you gain control over your financial future.

And when you give up the search for certainty, an enormous burden is lifted from your shoulders. You can begin to invest re-alistically, and that's much easier than the search for certainty.

## You Don't Have to Know Everything

Not only do you know very little, you don't *need* to know very much, or to spend a great deal of time dealing with your investments. You can take care of yourself—even though your understanding, time, and knowledge are limited—as long as you have a Permanent Portfolio.

In fact, the less you know—and the more honestly you recognize the limits of your knowledge—the more likely your investment program will turn out okay.

Humility is accepting that you don't know everything, or even everything about any particular topic, and it is an investor's most vital asset. Arrogance eventually ruins any investor who thinks he's found the Rosetta stone—the secret decoder that will beat the market—no matter how well he does for a while.

We recognize our limitations in other areas of life. You sometimes depend on systems and people you don't know much about. But when doing so puts you in danger— physically, emotionally, or financially—you simply back off and look for a safer course of action.

The investment markets are no different from the rest of life. You just need to apply to investing the same common sense you use already. Don't expect mysterious principles that make no sense elsewhere to work in the investment markets.

## What You Have

Once you have a Permanent Portfolio, you'll be free to enjoy your life—a good deal freer than other investors are. You also will be freer to speculate if you want to, because the Permanent Portfolio provides a safety net beneath you.

Although the Permanent Portfolio gives you the security of an insurance policy, it's better than insurance—because it doesn't cost you anything. Safety doesn't come at the expense of growth. In fact, over the period of your working life, you probably will earn a much better return on your Permanent Portfolio than many people achieve with complicated investment programs.

It's true that someone's investments will outperform your portfolio this year. And someone else's investments will outperform you next year. You may never have a year in which you're #1. But, most likely, each year it will be a different group of people who outperform you. And few investors will outperform your Permanent Portfolio over any stretch of years.

## You're on Your Own

So now it's time to wrap this up.

What final advice could I give you—to take care of you when you're out on your own?

Simply to remind you of Rule #17: *When in doubt about an investment decision, it is always better to err on the side of safety.*

In this uncertain world, whenever the choices before you aren't clear-cut, take the safest route. True, you might miss out on an opportunity that someone else exploits. But then, you might also miss out on a chance to lose everything you have.

Every day, someone will make more money than you do. But that doesn't mean you should have done what he did. He did what he thought best for himself. You must do what you think is best for you—considering your natural talents, your acquired skills, your knowledge, your interests, and the other things you need to attend to.

Investing isn't terrifying—so long as you don't think you

have to prove something, so long as all you care about is ensuring that your future is safe.

No one has decreed that you must be a big winner in the market.

You don't have to be courageous; you don't have to emulate the masters of finance. If you come up against something you don't want to do with your investments, don't do it. When your stomach says no, obey it.

Pay no attention to advice that you can survive financially only by becoming a speculator—or short seller, option trader, international expert, ballet dancer, whatever. There's nothing that everyone must be. There are eager, ambitious people—with a feel for speculation—who have tried to carry out sophisticated plans and have lost heavily. Someone who's reluctant or untrained or with no talent for speculating has almost no chance at all.

So whenever someone pressures you to strike while the iron is hot, to be something you aren't, to take a chance that seems dangerous, remember:

*When in doubt about an investment decision, it is always better to err on the side of safety.*

Thank you for spending this time with me. I wish you the very best.

Nashville, Tennessee, June 14, 1999

# Appendices

# Appendix A:
# Acknowledgments

Although I entered the investment business in 1967 and was fortunate to enjoy a good deal of success, my current understanding of investment strategy began to develop when I met Terry Coxon in 1974.

I have believed since childhood that we live in an uncertain world. With Terry's help I began to see how it was possible to find both safety and profit in such a world. Since 1974 he has contributed something valuable to almost everything I've written, including this book. His understanding of economics and good writing have been indispensable to me, and there's no way I can thank him enough.

This is the book I've been leading up to for thirty years,

and it probably will be my final investment book. So I'm grateful to St. Martin's Press and editor George Witte for publishing it.

The book relies especially on ideas that were developed during the writing of my newsletter from 1974 to 1997. So I'm thankful that John Chandler and Charles Smith undertook to publish the newsletter through which my ideas could be expressed and evolve.

Most of all, my wife, Pamela, has always provided the greatest encouragement and support.

# Appendix B:
# Where to Get Help

This appendix describes some products, services, and companies that may help you with the investments needed for a Permanent Portfolio or help you better understand the possibilities available to you.

There undoubtedly are many useful sources that aren't listed here. I've included only those with which I have some acquaintance or that are known nationally.

Except where I've indicated otherwise, I have no financial interest in any of these firms—except perhaps as a customer.

Needless to say, I can't control what anyone does. So I can't guarantee the success of your relationship with any source mentioned here. You'll have to evaluate each of them as you would any stranger. They're listed here not as recommendations, but to save you from having to hunt for them.

## Stock Market Mutual Funds

Here are eight mutual funds that fulfill the qualifications I gave on page 108. With the exception of adding the Aggressive Growth Portfolio (which began operating in 1991), I haven't altered my choices since first selecting the funds in 1987. I don't think you should replace a fund unless it loses its character and becomes unsuitable for the portfolio. Chasing performance is a losing game.

Use at least three different funds, in case any fund fails to capitalize on a bull market. Contact the funds for full information and application forms. Each is available in all states.

Aggressive Growth Portfolio
Permanent Portfolio Family of Funds[1]
1601 West 38th Street, Suite 207
Austin, Texas 78731
TELEPHONE: (800) 531-5142, (512) 453-7313
FAX: (512) 453-2015
E-MAIL: None
WORLD WIDE WEB ADDRESS: None
MINIMUM INITIAL PURCHASE: $1,000

---

[1] I am a consultant to the Permanent Portfolio Family of Funds.

American Century Growth Fund
(formerly Twentieth Century Growth Investors)
4500 Main Street
P.O. Box 419200
Kansas City, Missouri 64141
TELEPHONE: (800) 345-2021, (816) 531-5575
FAX: None
E-MAIL: None
WORLD WIDE WEB ADDRESS: www.AmericanCentury.com
MINIMUM PURCHASE: $2,500 (IRA, $1,000; Keogh, $0)

Columbia Growth Fund
1301 S.W. 5th Avenue
P.O. Box 1350
Portland, Oregon 97207-1350
TELEPHONE: (800) 547-1707; Fax (503) 222-3606
E-MAIL: Via website
WORLD WIDE WEB ADDRESS: www.ColumbiaFunds.com
MINIMUM INITIAL PURCHASE: $1,000

Evergreen Fund
Evergreen Keystone Service
P.O. Box 2121
Boston, Massachusetts 02106
TELEPHONE: (800) 343-2898, (617) 210-3200;
FAX: (617) 210-2711
E-MAIL: None
WORLD WIDE WEB ADDRESS: www.Evergreen-funds.com
MINIMUM INITIAL PURCHASE: $1,000 (IRA/Keogh, $0)

Manhattan Fund
Neuberger & Berman
605 Third Avenue
New York, New York 10158
TELEPHONE: (800) 877-9700, (212) 476-8800
FAX: None
E-MAIL: Questions@NBfunds.com
WORLD WIDE WEB ADDRESS: www.NBfunds.com
MINIMUM INITIAL PURCHASE: $1,000 (IRA/Keogh, $250)

Morgan Growth Fund
Vanguard Funds
P.O. Box 2600
Valley Forge, Pennsylvania 19482
TELEPHONE: (800) 662-2739, (215) 648-6000
FAX: None
E-MAIL: Online@Vanguard.com
WORLD WIDE WEB ADDRESS: www.vanguard.com
MINIMUM INITIAL PURCHASE: $3,000 (IRA/Keogh, $1,000)

Scudder Large Company Value Fund
(formerly Scudder Capital Growth Fund)
P.O. Box 2291
Boston, Massachusetts 02107-2291
TELEPHONE: (800) 225-5163, (617) 295-1000
FAX: None
E-MAIL: None
WORLD WIDE WEB ADDRESS: www.scudder.com
MINIMUM INITIAL PURCHASE: $2,500(IRA/Keogh, $500)

Tudor Fund
WPG (Weiss, Peck & Greer)
One New York Plaza
New York, New York 10004
TELEPHONE: (800) 223-3332, (212) 908-9500
FAX: None
E-MAIL: None
WORLD WIDE WEB ADDRESS: None
MINIMUM INITIAL PURCHASE: $2,500 (IRA/Keogh, $250)

## Treasury-Bill Money Market Funds Appropriate for a Permanent Portfolio

To be suitable for the Permanent Portfolio's cash portion, a money market fund should be 100% invested in Treasury securities, without using repurchase agreements as investments. All these funds qualify.[2]

American Century Preservation Fund
(formerly Capital Preservation Fund)
P.O. Box 419200
Kansas City, Missouri 64141
TELEPHONE: (800) 345-2021; (816) 531-5575
FAX: (816) 340-7962
E-MAIL: None
WORLD WIDE WEB ADDRESS: www.AmericanCentury.com
MINIMUM INVESTMENT: $2,500 (IRA, $1,000; Keogh, $0)

---

[2] Repurchase agreements are a method by which some money market funds enhance the return on their investments slightly by taking a slightly greater risk.

Dreyfus 100% U.S. Treasury Money Market Fund
200 Park Avenue
New York, New York 10166
TELEPHONE: (800) 373-9387, (718) 895-1206
FAX: None
E-MAIL: info@dreyfus.com
WORLD WIDE WEB ADDRESS: www.dreyfus.com
MINIMUM INVESTMENT: $2,500 (IRA/Keogh: $750)

Neuberger & Berman Government Money Fund, Inc.
342 Madison Avenue
New York, New York 10173
TELEPHONE: (800) 877-9700, (212) 850-8300
FAX: None
E-MAIL: Questions@NBfunds.com
WORLD WIDE WEB ADDRESS: www.NBfunds.com
MINIMUM INVESTMENT: $2,000 (IRA/Keogh: $250)

Treasury Bill Portfolio
Permanent Portfolio Family of Funds[3]
1601 West 38th Street, Suite 207
Austin, Texas 78731
TELEPHONE: (800) 531-5142, (512) 453-7313
FAX: (512) 453-2015
E-MAIL: None
WORLD WIDE WEB ADDRESS: None
MINIMUM INVESTMENT: $1,000 (IRA/Keogh: $1,000)

---

[3] The Treasury Bill Portfolio lets its share price rise—rather than fixing it at $1 per share and paying daily dividends. By minimizing the payment of dividends, the fund permits a portion of an investor's earnings to accumulate and compound without a tax liability until the shares are redeemed. I am a consultant to the Permanent Portfolio Family of Funds.

## Gold Coin Dealers

Gold coins are the most convenient and useful way to hold the gold portion of a Permanent Portfolio. They allow divisibility—making it easy for you to rebalance the portfolio with small purchases or sales whenever necessary.

Don't have any U.S. firm store the coins for you. Take care of that yourself, so you aren't dependent on anyone else's survival. A bank safe deposit box is a suitable storage place.

Buy "bullion coins"—coins whose price represents the gold content, rather than paying a premium of 10% or more for the rarity of the coin. American Eagle gold coins, the Canadian Maple Leaf, the South African Krugerrand, and the Austrian Philharmonic are all appropriate.

In addition to these dealers, there are some stockbrokers who sell gold coins.

Camino Coin Company
851 Burlway Road
Burlingame, California 94011
TELEPHONE: (800) 348-8001, (650) 348-3000
FAX: (650) 401-5530
E-MAIL: CaminoCoin@earthlink.net
WORLD WIDE WEB ADDRESS: www.CaminoCoin.com

Investment Rarities
7850 Metro Parkway
Minneapolis, Minnesota 55425
TELEPHONE: (800) 328-1860, (612) 853-0700
FAX: (612) 851-8732
E-MAIL: None
WORLD WIDE WEB ADDRESS: www.InvestmentRarities.com

Monex Deposit Company
4910 Birch Street
Newport Beach, California 92660
TELEPHONE: (800) 949-4653; (949) 752-1400
FAX: (949) 752-7214
E-MAIL: Monex@Monex.com
WORLD WIDE WEB ADDRESS: www.monex.com

## The Permanent Portfolio Fund

If you find the idea of setting up your own Permanent Portfolio too difficult, or if your capital is too small to diversify on your own, a tailor-made alternative is Terry Coxon's Permanent Portfolio Fund. The fund, established in 1981, keeps investments in permanent allocations without attempting to foresee the future or time the markets. Even if you have your own Permanent Portfolio, or intend to set one up, the Permanent Portfolio Fund can be a supplement to your own portfolio—a way of making additions and withdrawals conveniently without disrupting your fixed percentages—or it can protect you until you have the opportunity to arrange your own portfolio.

The Permanent Portfolio Fund
Permanent Portfolio Family of Funds[4]
1601 West 38th Street, Suite 207
Austin, Texas 78731
TELEPHONE: (800) 531-5142, (512) 453-7313

---

[4] I am a consultant to the Permanent Portfolio Family of Funds.

FAX: (512) 453-2015
E-MAIL: None
WORLD WIDE WEB ADDRESS: None
MINIMUM INITIAL PURCHASE: $1,000

## Foreign Banks

Here are four banks that can buy and store precious metals for you, as well as handle other investments. All of them are Swiss or Austrian, and are bound by the laws of those countries—not the countries of their parent companies.

Anglo-Irish Bank (Austria)
Rathausstrasse 20, P.O. Box 306
A-1011 Vienna, Austria
TELEPHONE: (011-431) 406-6161; Fax (011-431)
405-8142
E-MAIL: Welcome.desk@AngloIrishBank.at
WORLD WIDE WEB ADDRESS: www.AngloIrishBank.ie
CONTACTS: Peter Zipper, Karin Stoehr
MINIMUM TO OPEN ACCOUNT: US$5,000
ASSETS: 4 billion Austrian schillings (approx. US$341 million)

Anker Bank
Case postale 159
50, Av. de la Gare
CH-1001 Lausanne, Switzerland
TELEPHONE: (011-4121) 321-0707;
Fax (011-4121) 323-9767

E-MAIL: None
WORLD WIDE WEB ADDRESS: None
CONTACTS: Mr. Imfeld Jacques, Mr. Jean-Marc Del Custode
MINIMUM TO OPEN ACCOUNT: US$10,000
ASSETS: 1,200 million Swiss francs (approx. US$800 million)

Canadian Imperial Bank of Commerce (Switzerland) Ltd.
Lintheschergasse 15
P. O. Box 7476
CH-8023 Zürich, Switzerland
TELEPHONE: (011-4121) 215-6087;
Fax (011-411) 215-6008
E-MAIL: Schwarw@cibc.ca
WORLD WIDE WEB ADDRESS: None
CONTACTS: Mr. Werner W. Schwarz, Mrs. Roswith Eisenring
MINIMUM TO OPEN ACCOUNT: No minimum
ASSETS: 987 million Swiss francs (approx. US$662 million)

UeberseeBank
Limmatquai 2
CH-8024 Zürich, Switzerland
TELEPHONE: (011-411) 267-5555; Fax (011-411) 252-0447
E-MAIL: Mgonseth@aigpb.com or Rlengacher@aigpb.com
WORLD WIDE WEB ADDRESS: None
CONTACTS: Mr. Markus Gonseth, Mr. Robert Lengacher, Mr. Bruno Benz
MINIMUM TO OPEN ACCOUNT: US$5,000
ASSETS: 562 million Swiss francs (approx. US$393 million)

## Financial Planning

Terry Coxon
Private Investors
Box 2657
Petaluma, California 94953
TELEPHONE: (707) 778-1000; Fax (707) 778-8804
E-MAIL: 110072.2223@CompuServe.com
Terry Coxon has helped me since 1974, including helping
me develop the material in this book. If you need
assistance constructing a complete financial plan
(including tax planning, estate planning, and lawsuit
protection) around a Permanent Portfolio, you can
arrange an appointment for a consultation.

## Publications by Harry Browne and Others

LiamWorks
P.O. Box 2165
Great Falls, Montana 59403-2165
TELEPHONE: (888) 377-0417 (toll-free) or (406) 761-4806
FAX: (406) 453-1092
E-MAIL: FrontDesk@LiamWorks.com
WORLD WIDE WEB ADDRESS: www.HarryBrowne.com
This publisher carries publications I've written that
provide more details of the Permanent Portfolio, as well
as other publications on economics, government, and
self-improvement. Anything I've written that's still in
print can be obtained here.

*The Handbook for No-Load Fund Investors*
P.O. Box 318
Irvington-on-Hudson, New York 10533
TELEPHONE: (800) 252-2042, (914) 693-7420
FAX: (914) 693-8067
E-MAIL: NoLoadFund@aol.com
WORLD WIDE WEB ADDRESS: www.SheldonJacobs.com
The *Handbook* is a very helpful guide to selecting mutual funds. The 1999 edition describes 1,582 stock funds and 320 money market funds. (It also covers 669 bond funds.) It gives information on investment policies, as well as providing performance information for the past ten years. The price is $45.

*Hulbert Financial Digest*
5051-B Backlick Road
Annandale, Virginia 22003
TELEPHONE: (703) 750-9060; Fax (703) 750-9220
E-MAIL: HFD@HulbertDigest.com
WORLD WIDE WEB ADDRESS: www.HulbertDigest.com
The *Digest* is a monthly newsletter that keeps track of the model portfolios of several hundred investment newsletters, and reports on their performance. Although the *Digest* might not be as skeptical as I am about the ability of an advisor to beat the market, the results it reports do provide a dose of reality to those who have high hopes. A one-year subscription is $59.

*Keep What You Earn* by Terry Coxon
Times Books, $25
This book describes in detail many strategies—some simple, some complicated—for reducing the tax burden

on your investments. It is an excellent source for
learning about the available alternatives. It can be
obtained through all book outlets or by calling (800)
531-5142.

"The Untax Promise" by Daniel J. Pilla
Winning Publications, Inc.
2372 Leibel Street
St. Paul, Minnesota 55110
(800) 346-6829
$8
This short report refutes most of the arguments that
claim you don't have to file an income tax return or pay
income tax. If you should be persuaded by someone that
you can evade the income tax completely, please don't
put yourself in jeopardy without reading this report first.

# The Author

Harry Browne has been an investment consultant, radio personality, and public speaker—and in 1996 he was the Libertarian Party's candidate for President of the United States. This is his eleventh book.

He was born in New York City in 1933 and grew up in Los Angeles. He graduated from high school, but attended college for only two weeks. He has lived in California, Canada, and Switzerland. He now resides in Tennessee.

Browne's first two investment books—*How You Can Profit from the Coming Devaluation* in 1970 and *You Can Profit from a Monetary Crisis* in 1974—were best-sellers that helped thousands of investors profit from the turmoil of the inflationary 1970s.

In 1973 he published *How I Found Freedom in an Unfree World*, an unusual self-help book still in demand today. A 25th anniversary edition with a new Foreword and Afterword was published in 1998.

His financial newsletter, *Harry Browne's Special Reports*, was published from 1974 to 1997. He now is retired from the investment business.

He is in constant demand for speeches and radio and TV interviews, and is widely respected for his honest, plain-spoken writing and investment advice.

Since 1985 Browne has been married to the former Pamela Lanier Wolfe. He has one daughter. His main non-professional interests are classical music, good food and wine, sports, and drama.